A VERY GROOVY COLORING BOOK

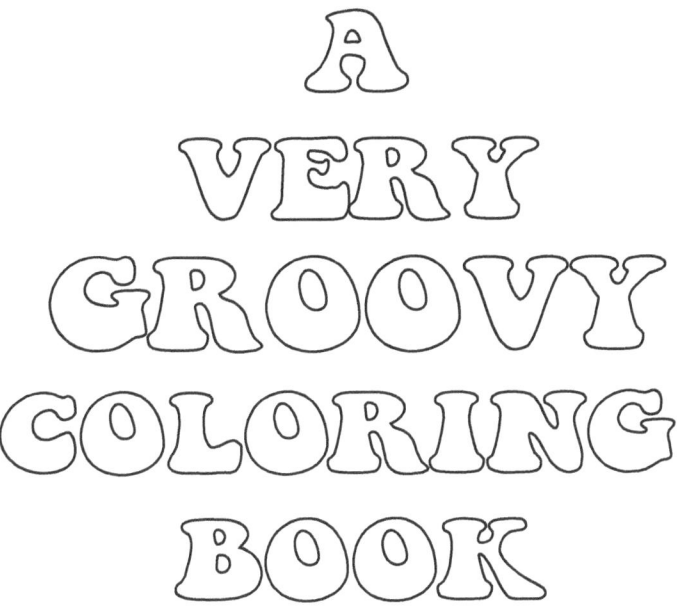

20 Designs for Good Vibes

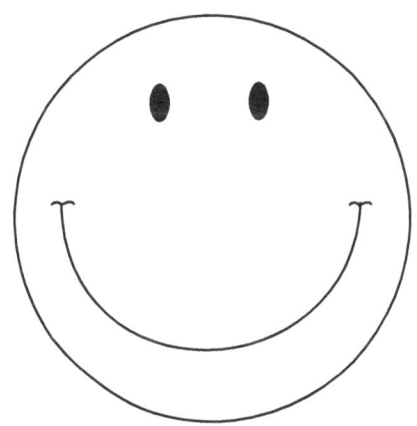

Illustrated by *Angele Jeanne*

A to Z Books

www.from-a-to-z.com

-Dedicated to my Aunt Dernice...
gone, but never forgotten.

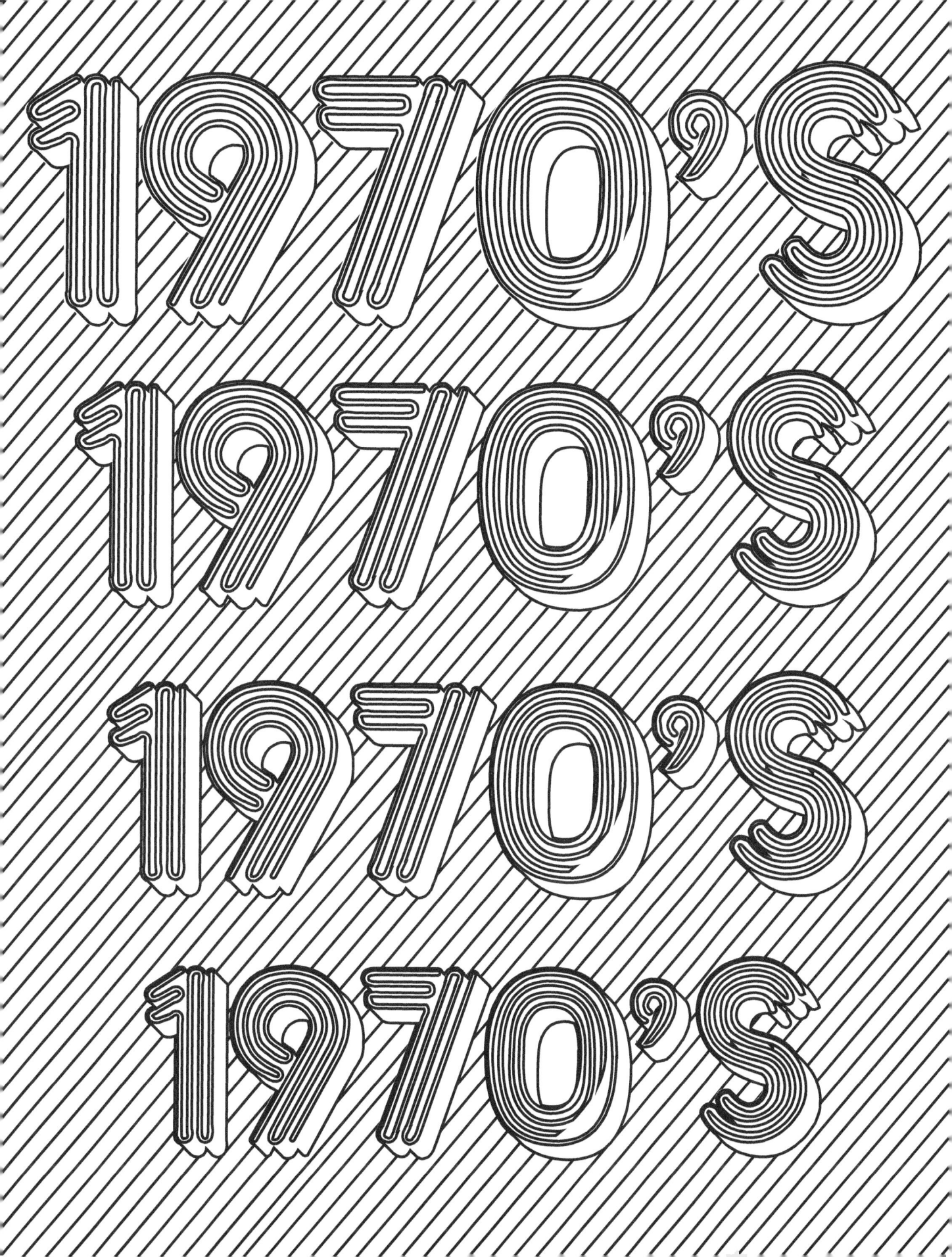

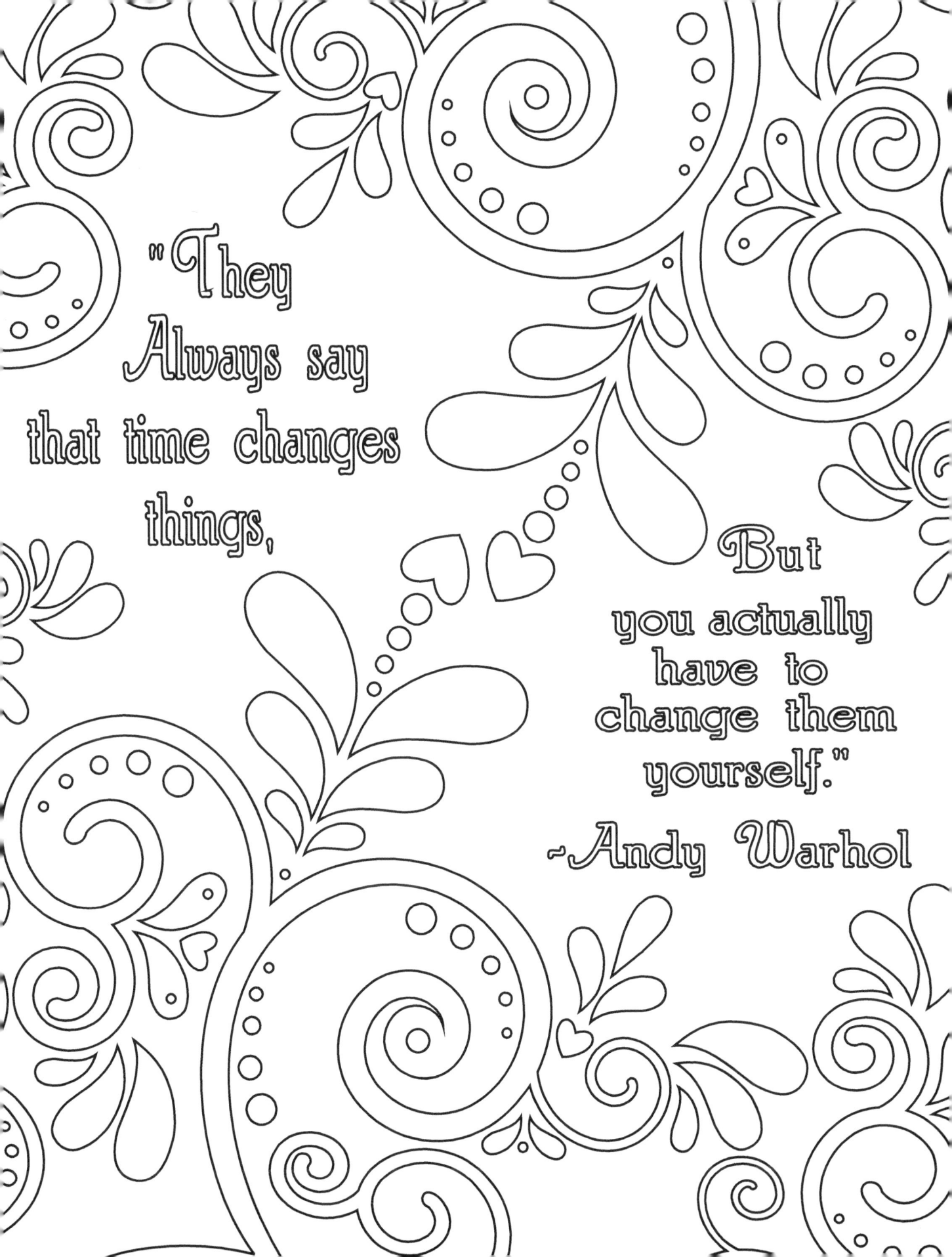

"They Always say that time changes things,

But you actually have to change them yourself."

~Andy Warhol

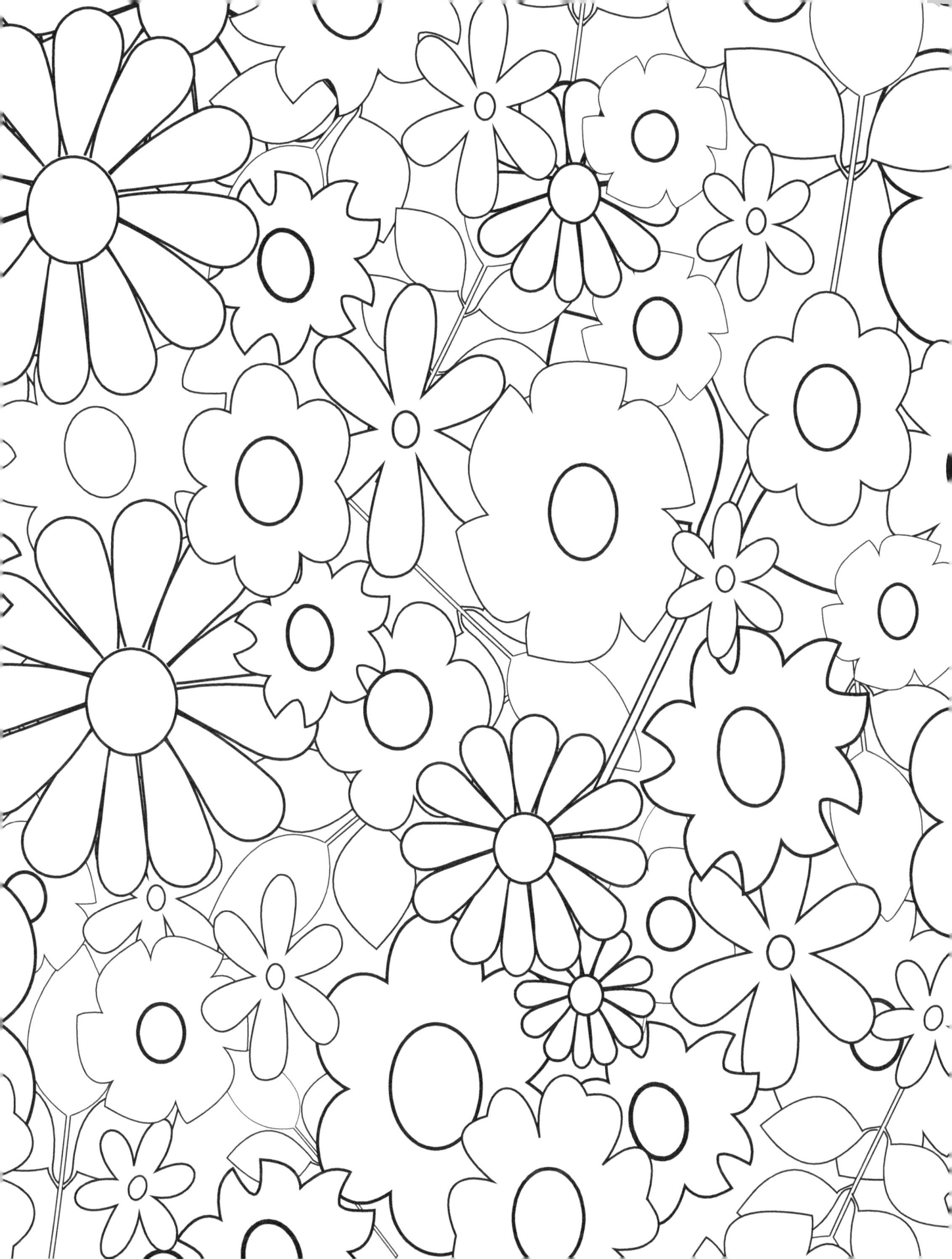

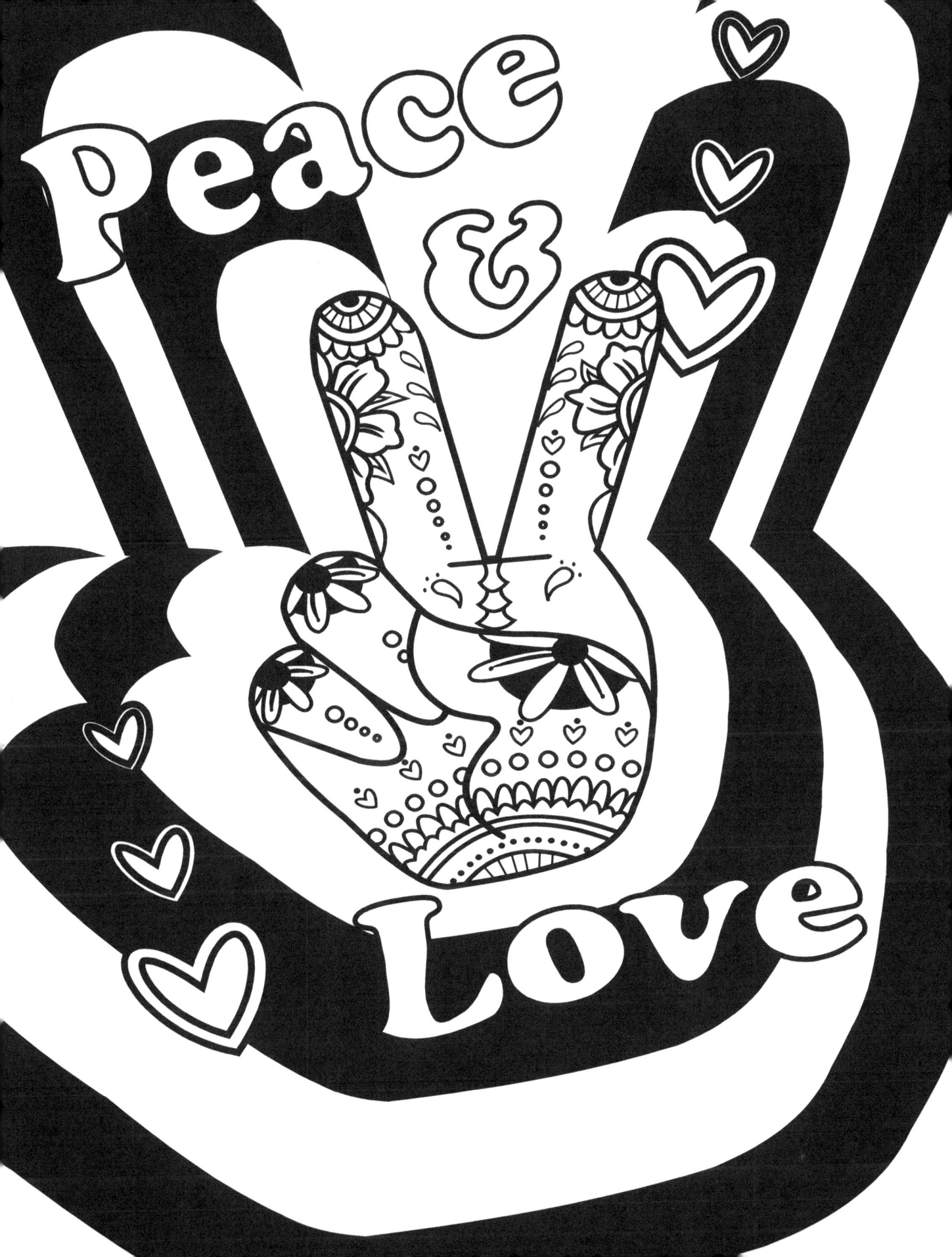

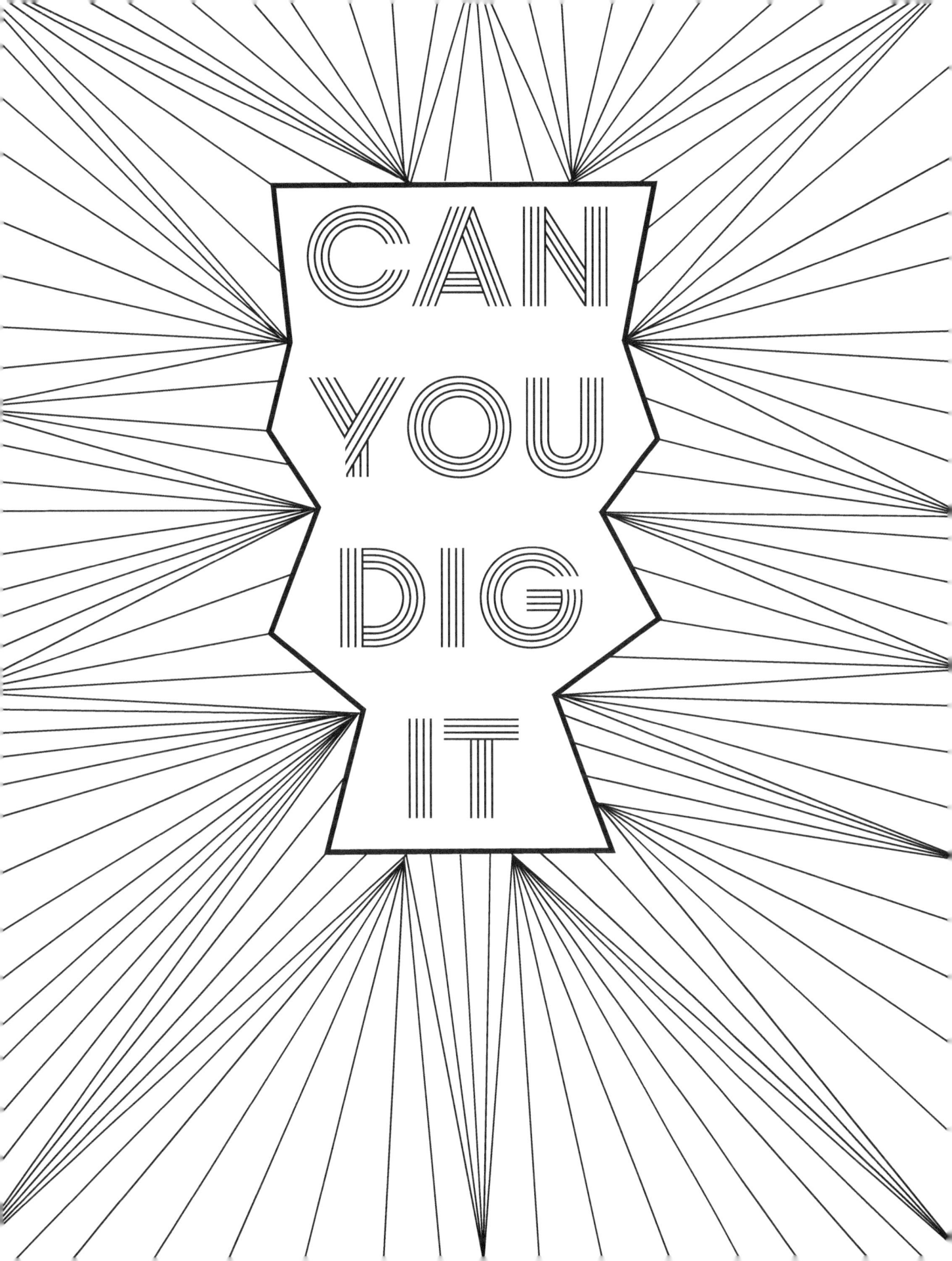

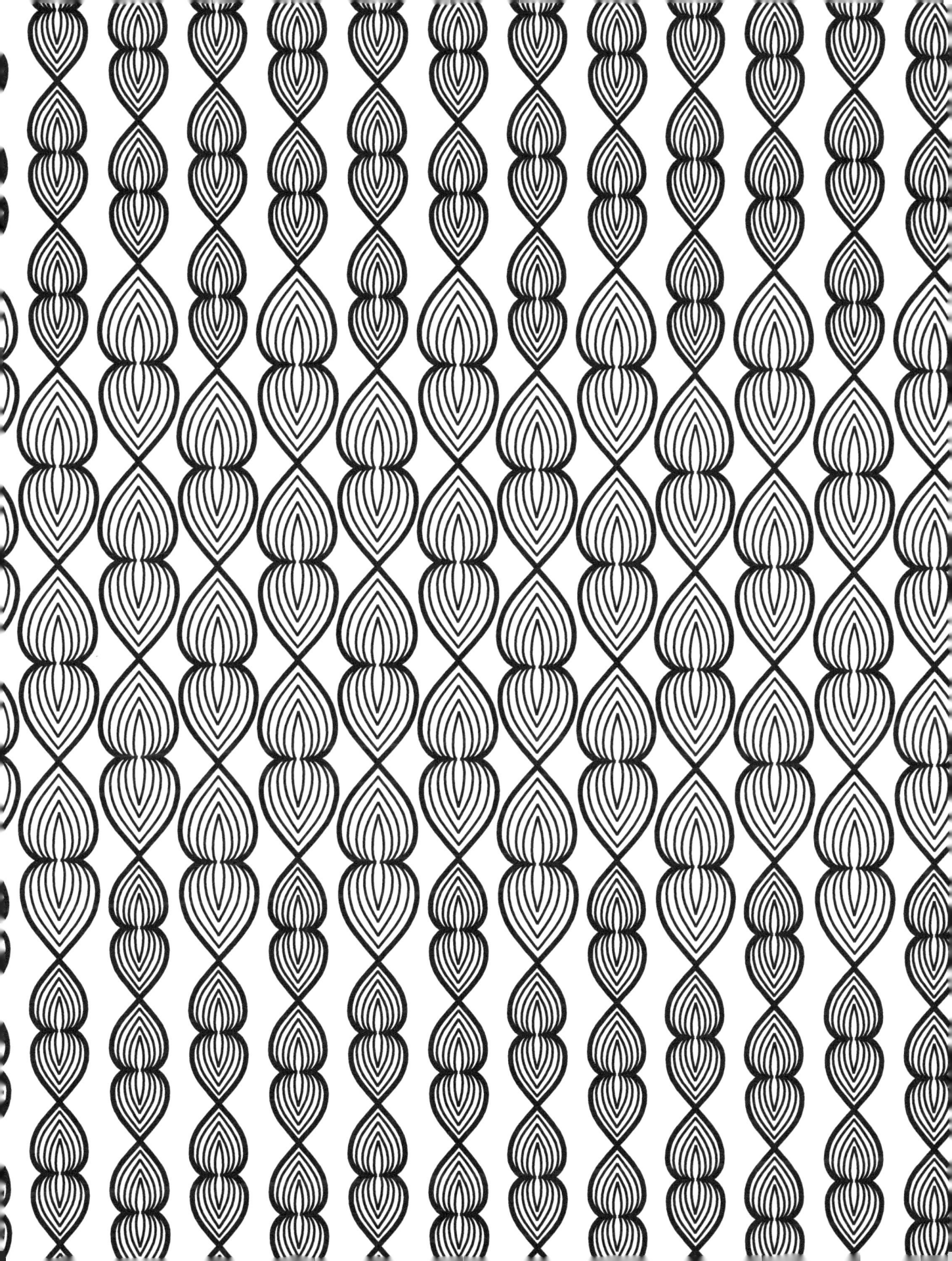

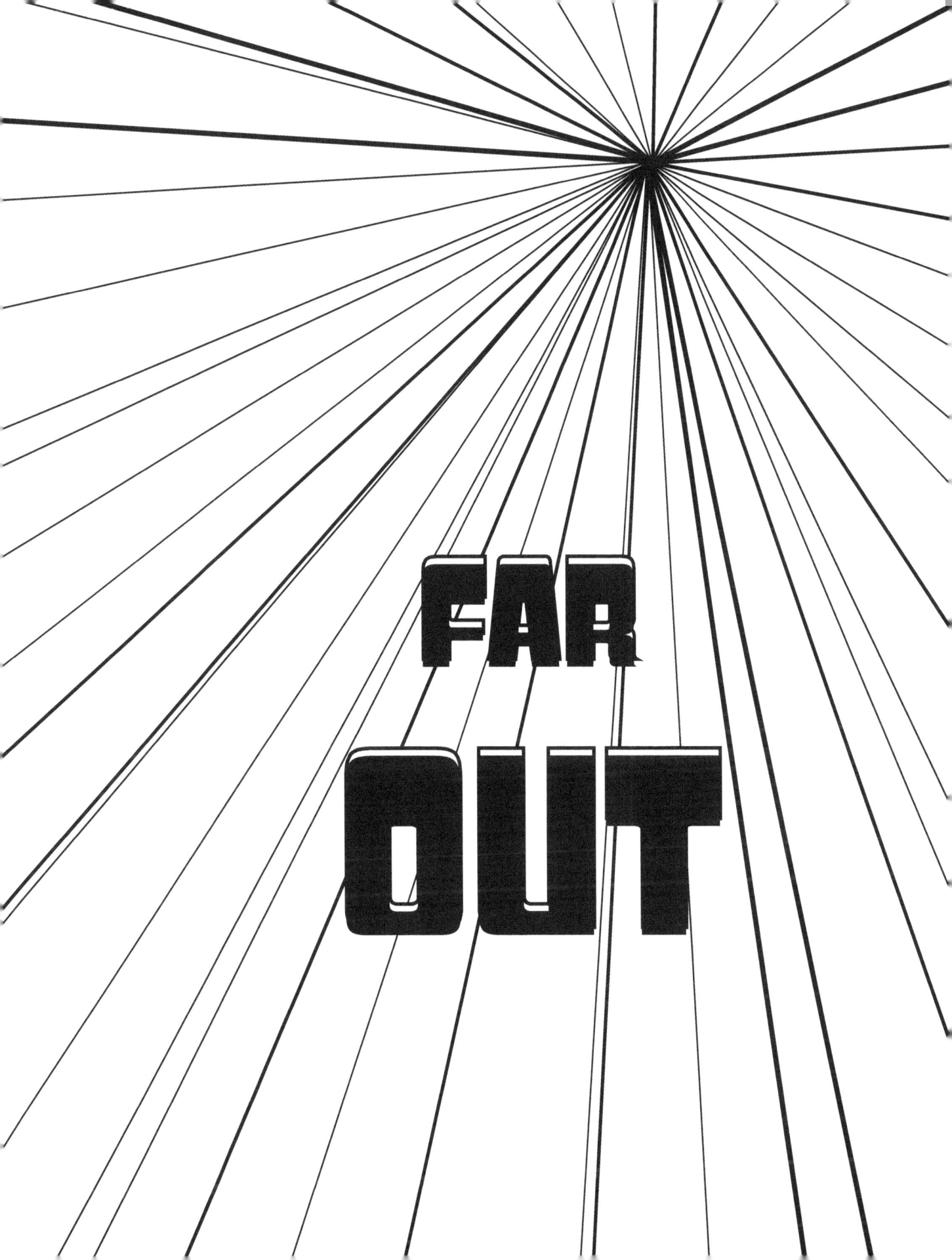

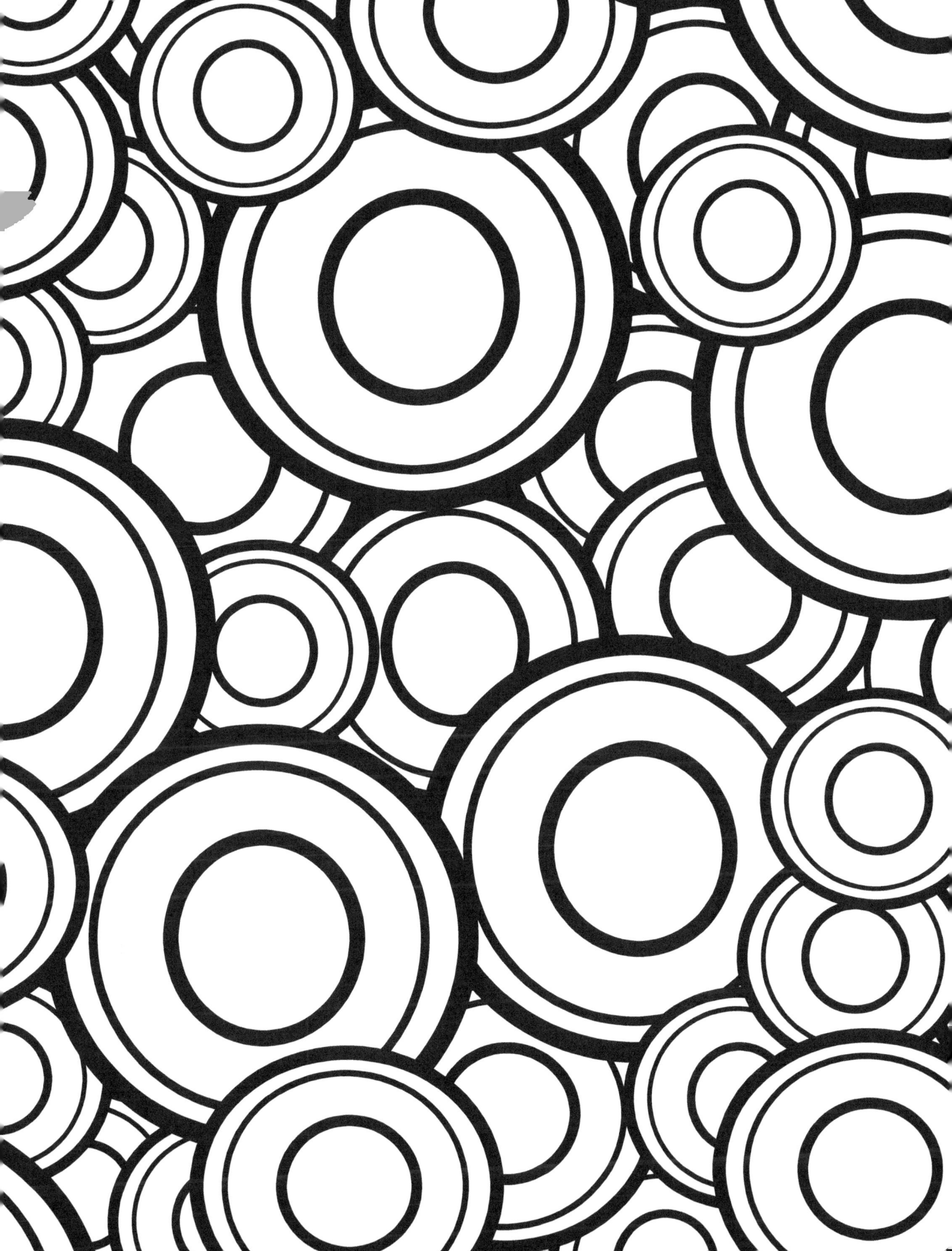

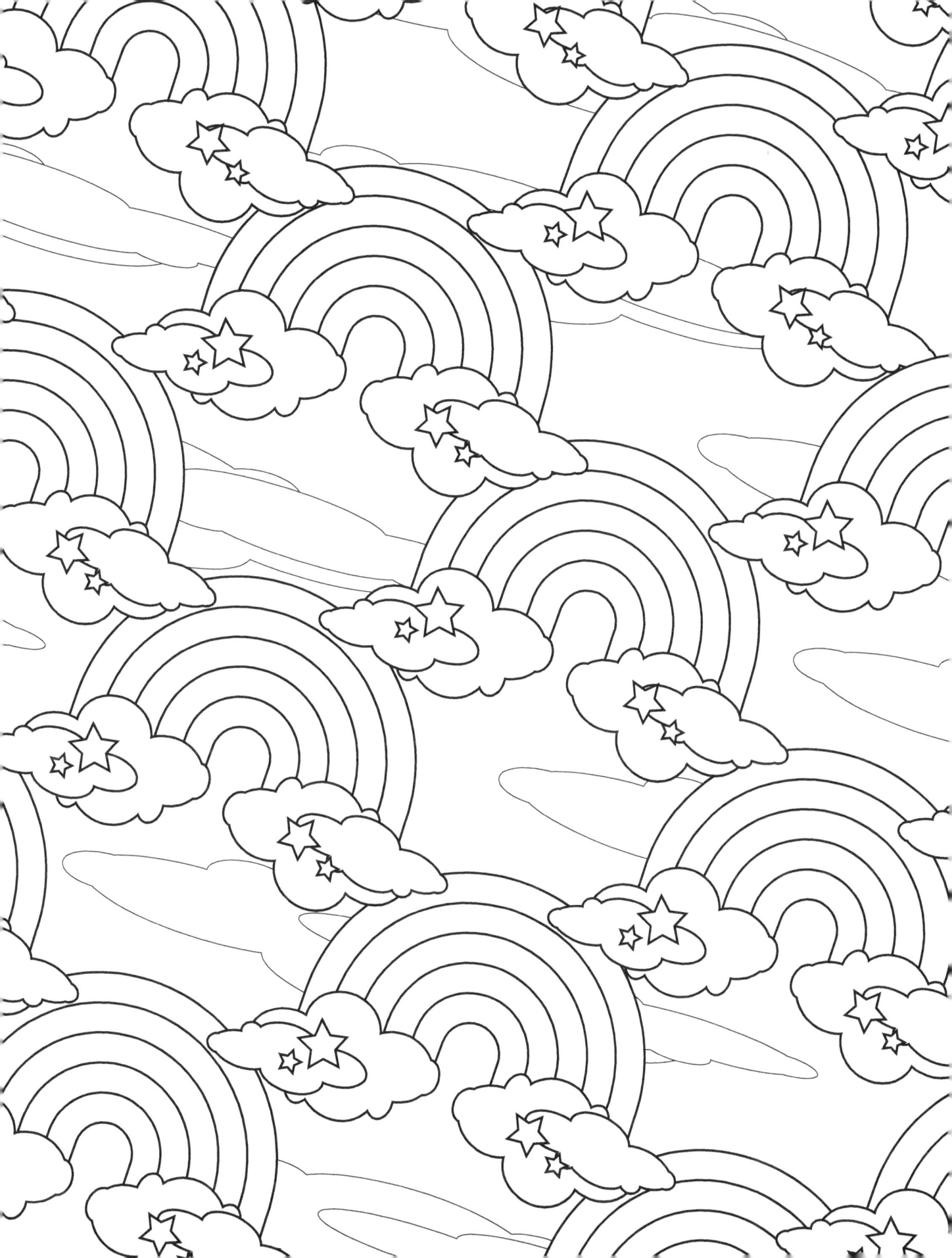

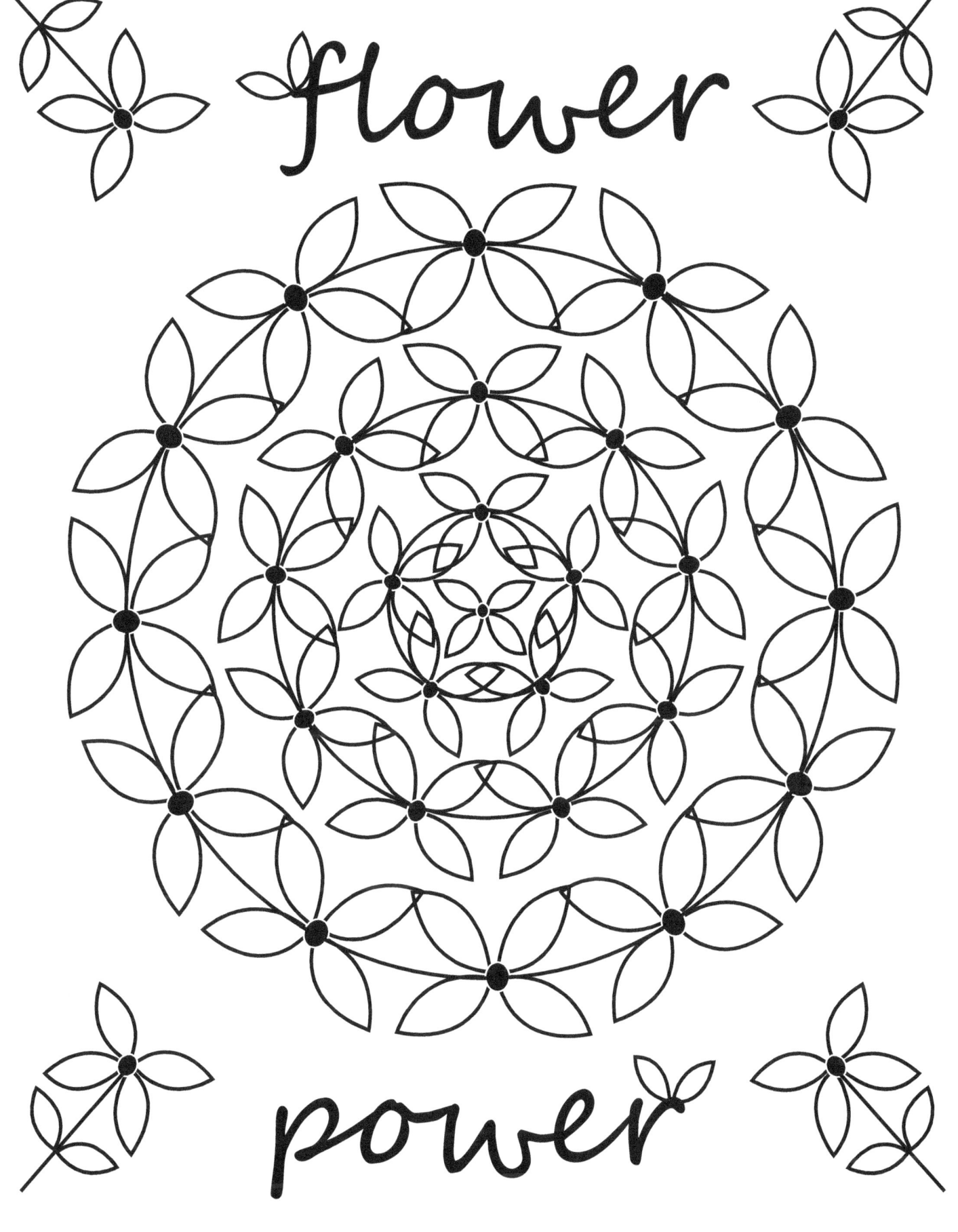

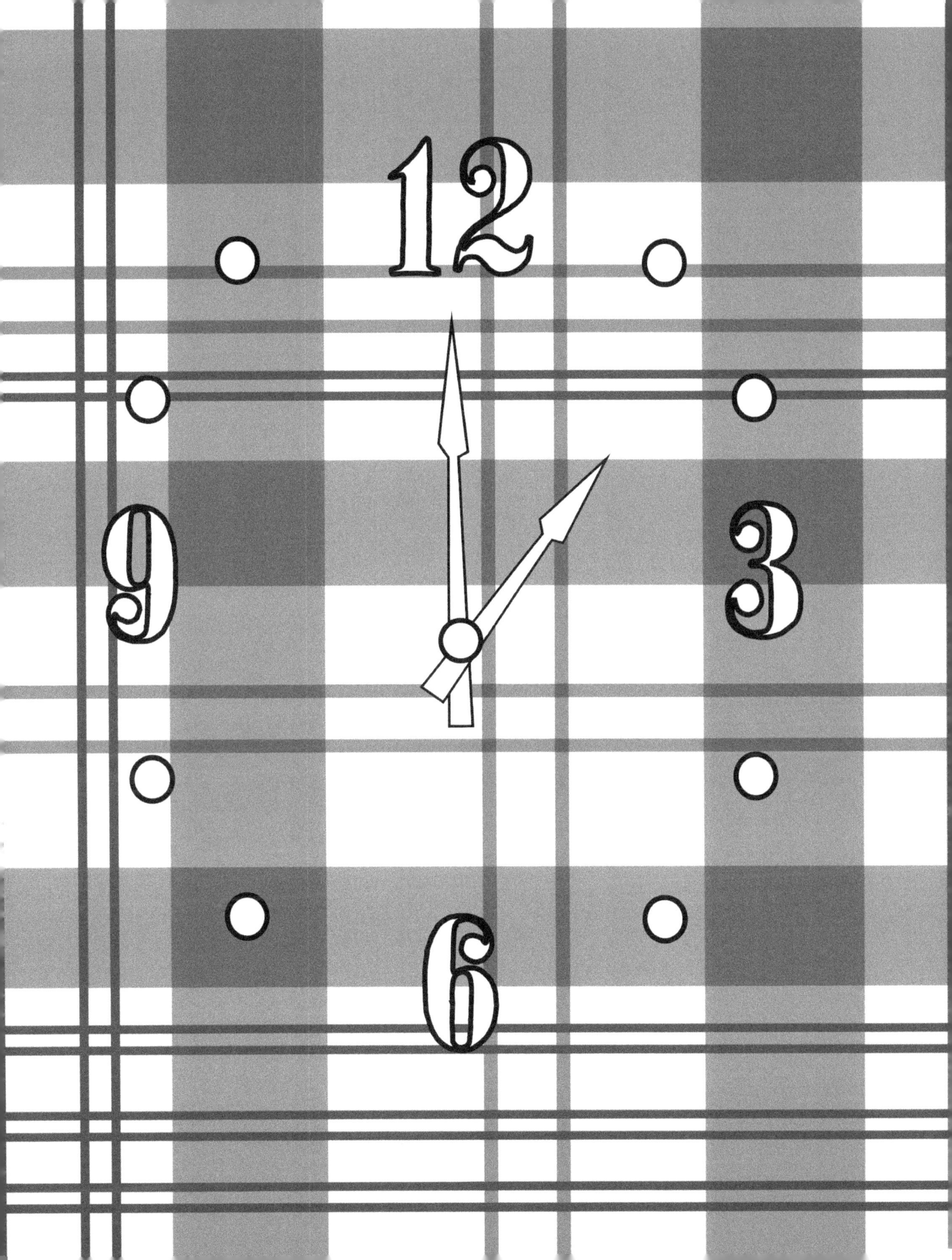

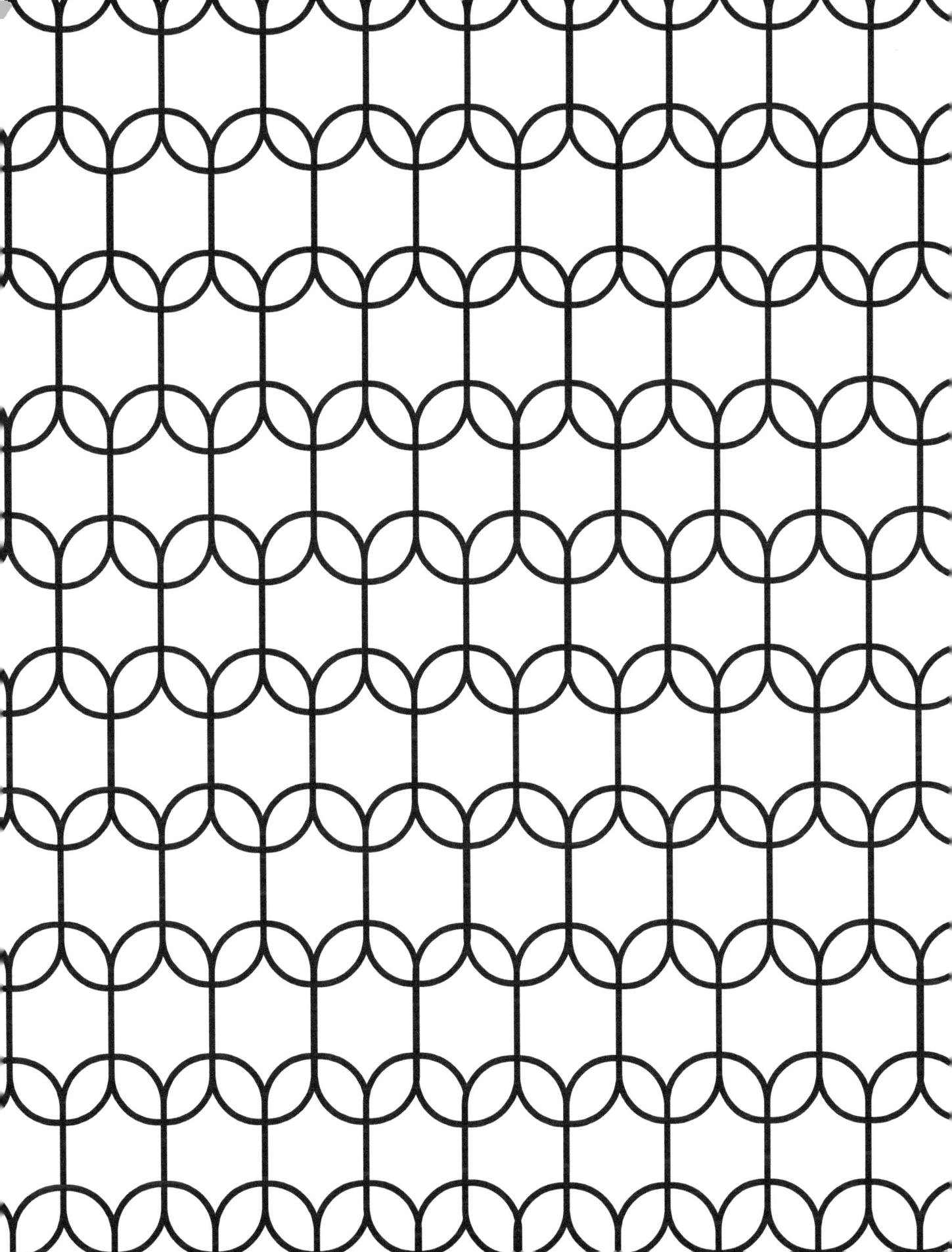

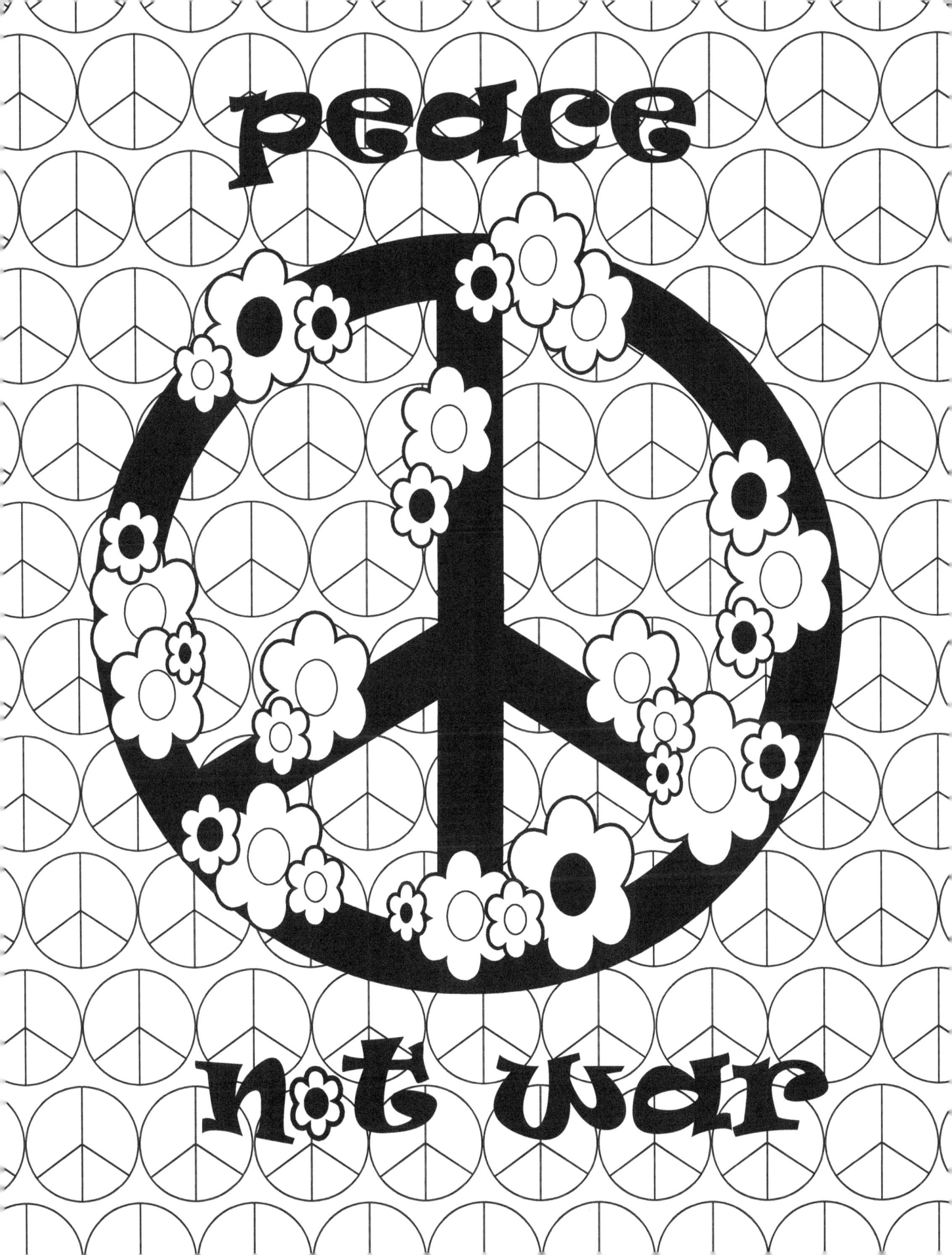

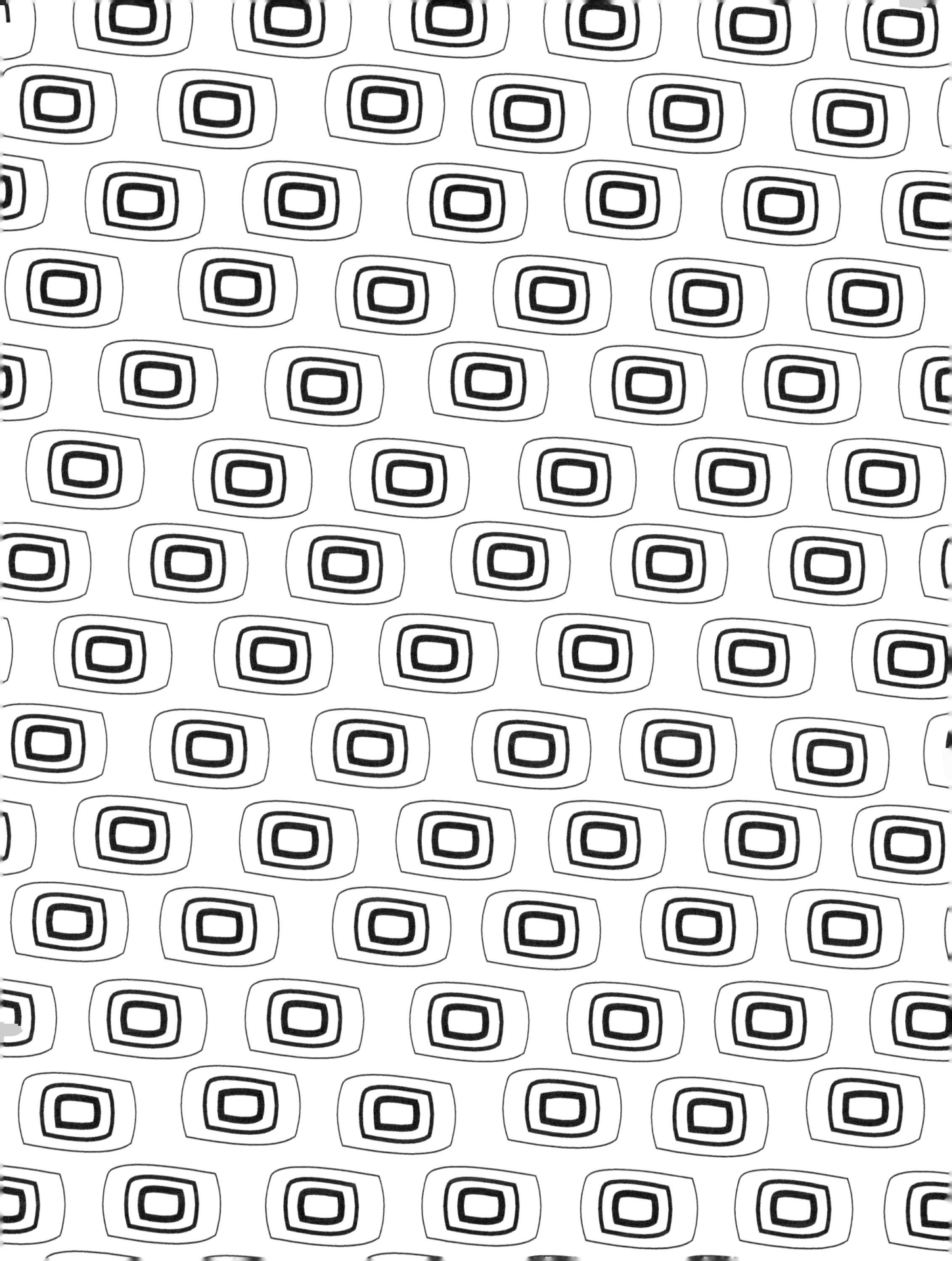

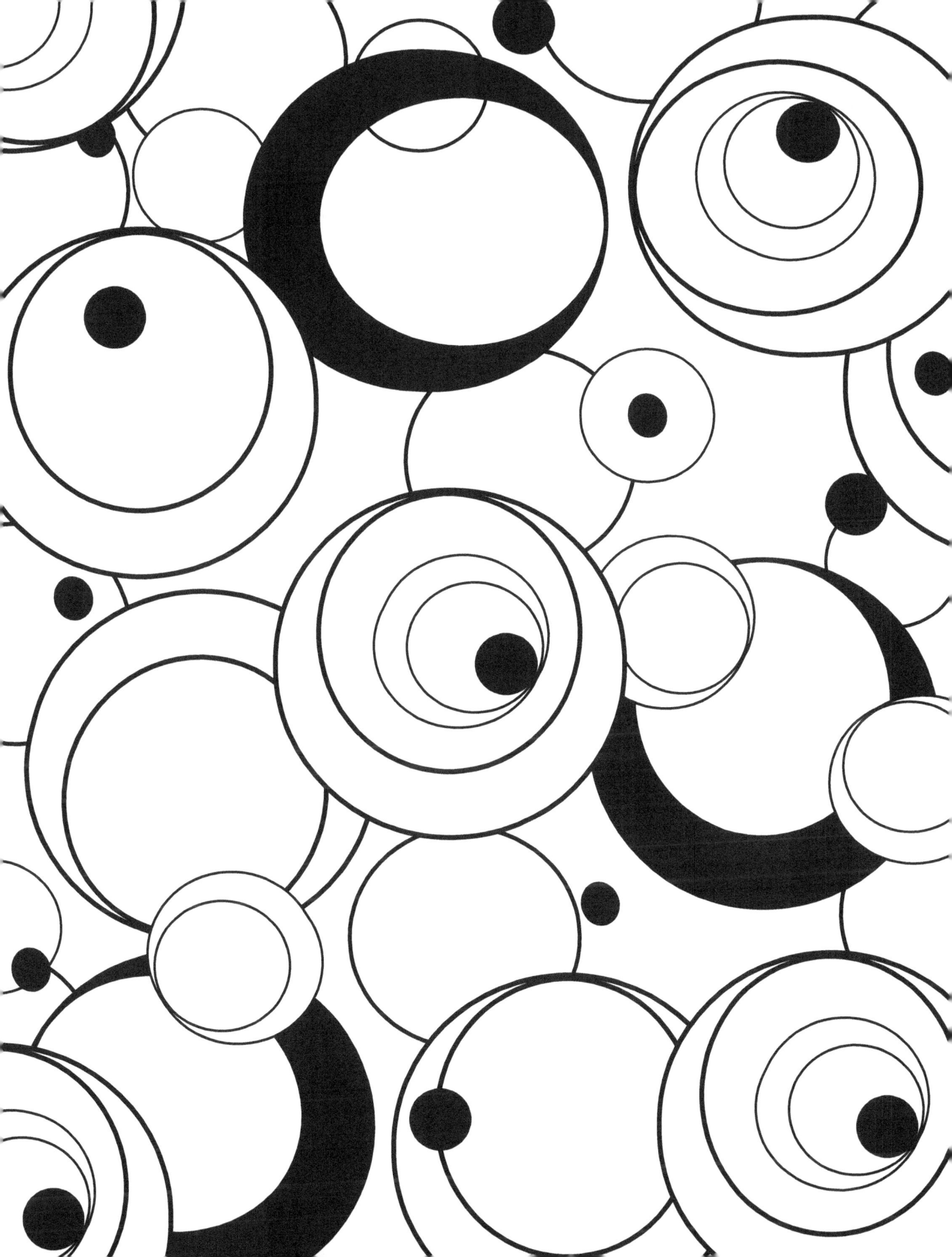

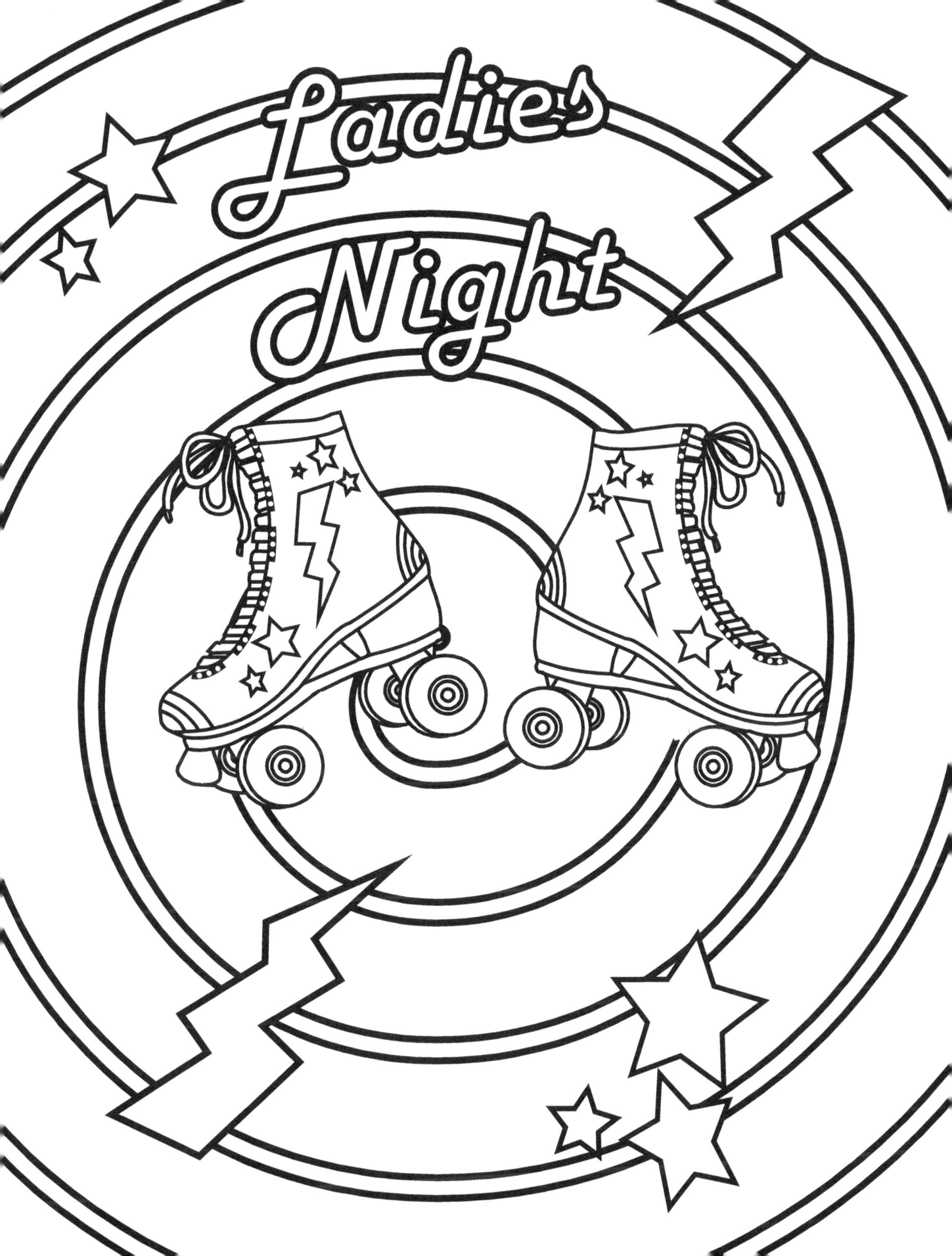

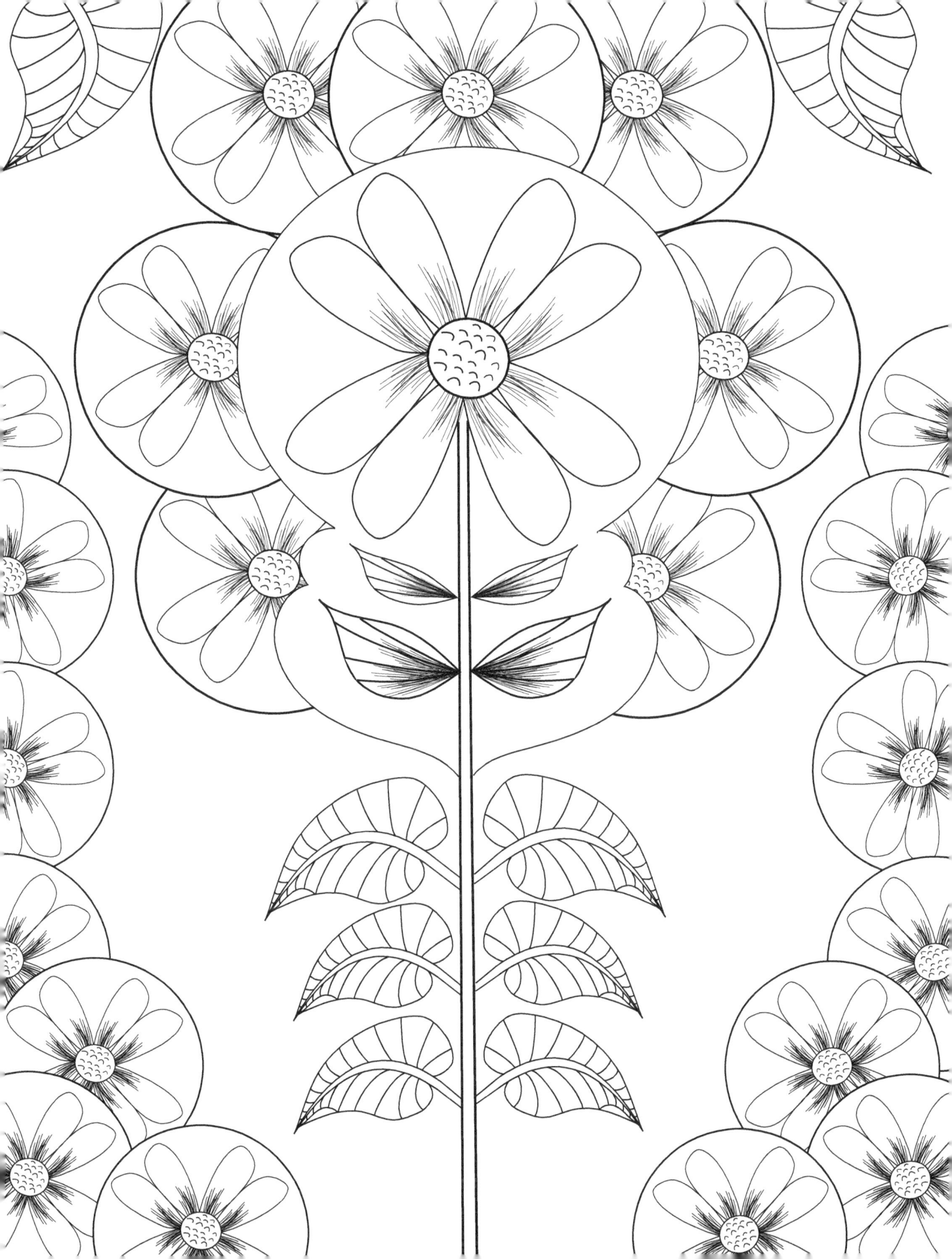

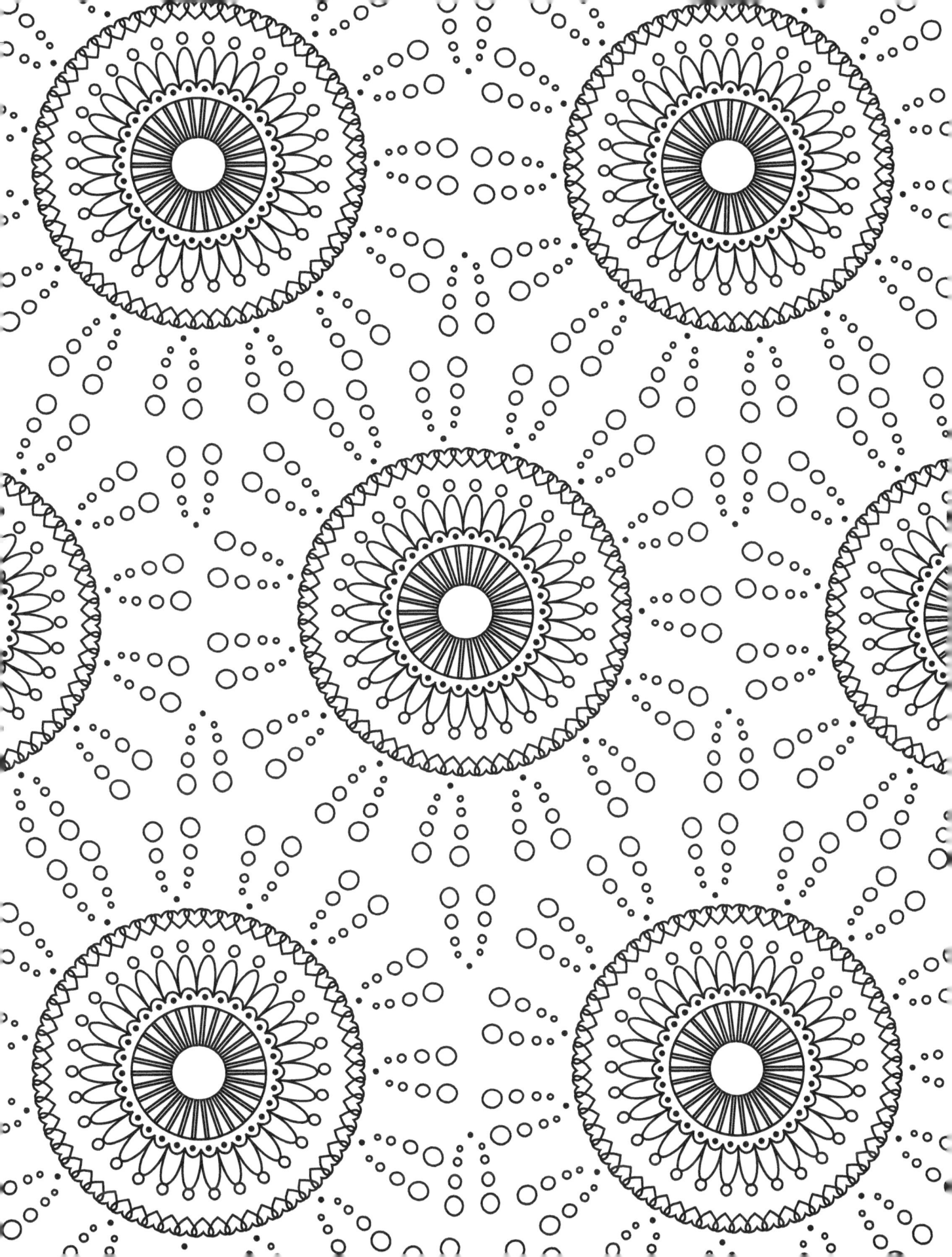

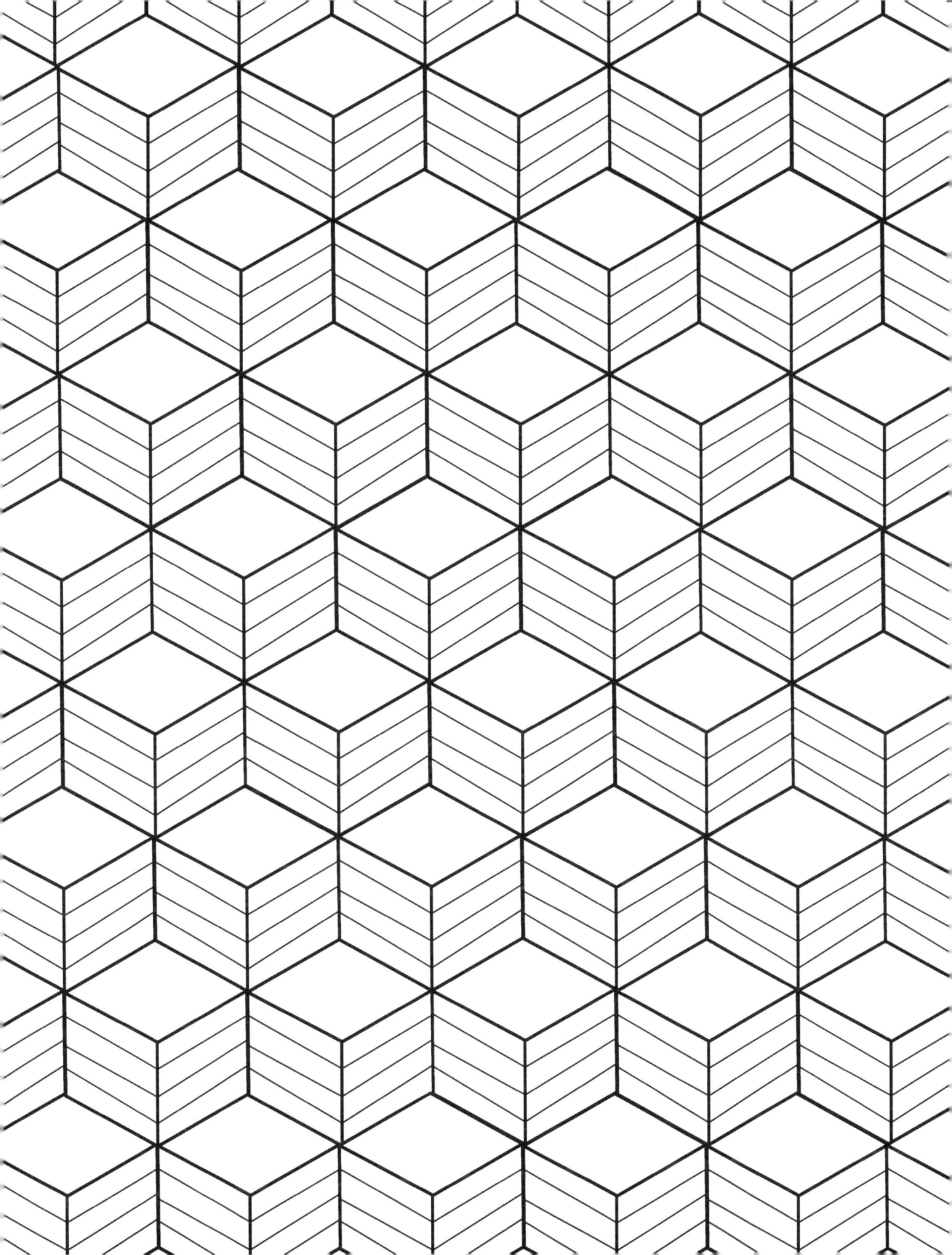

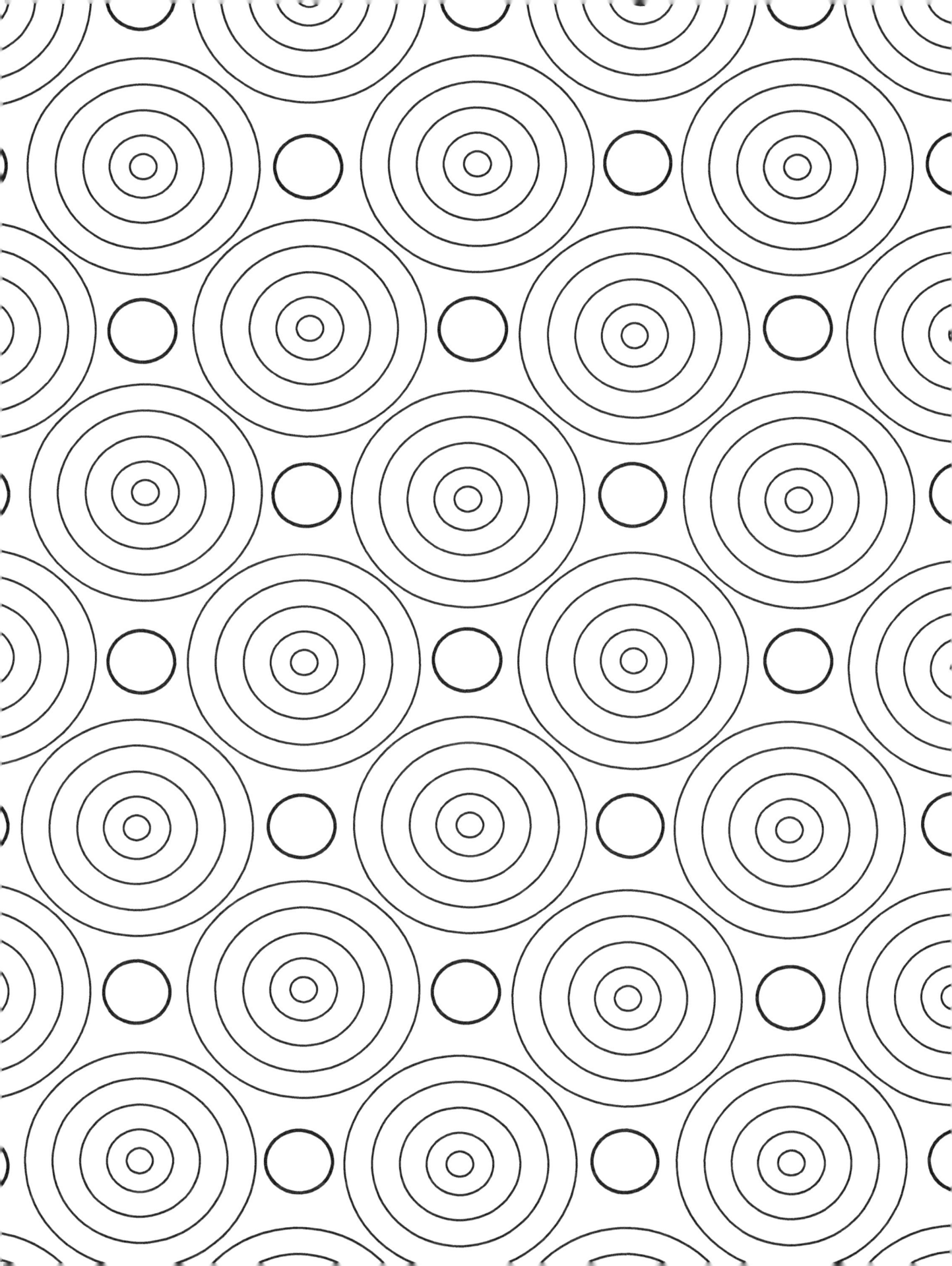

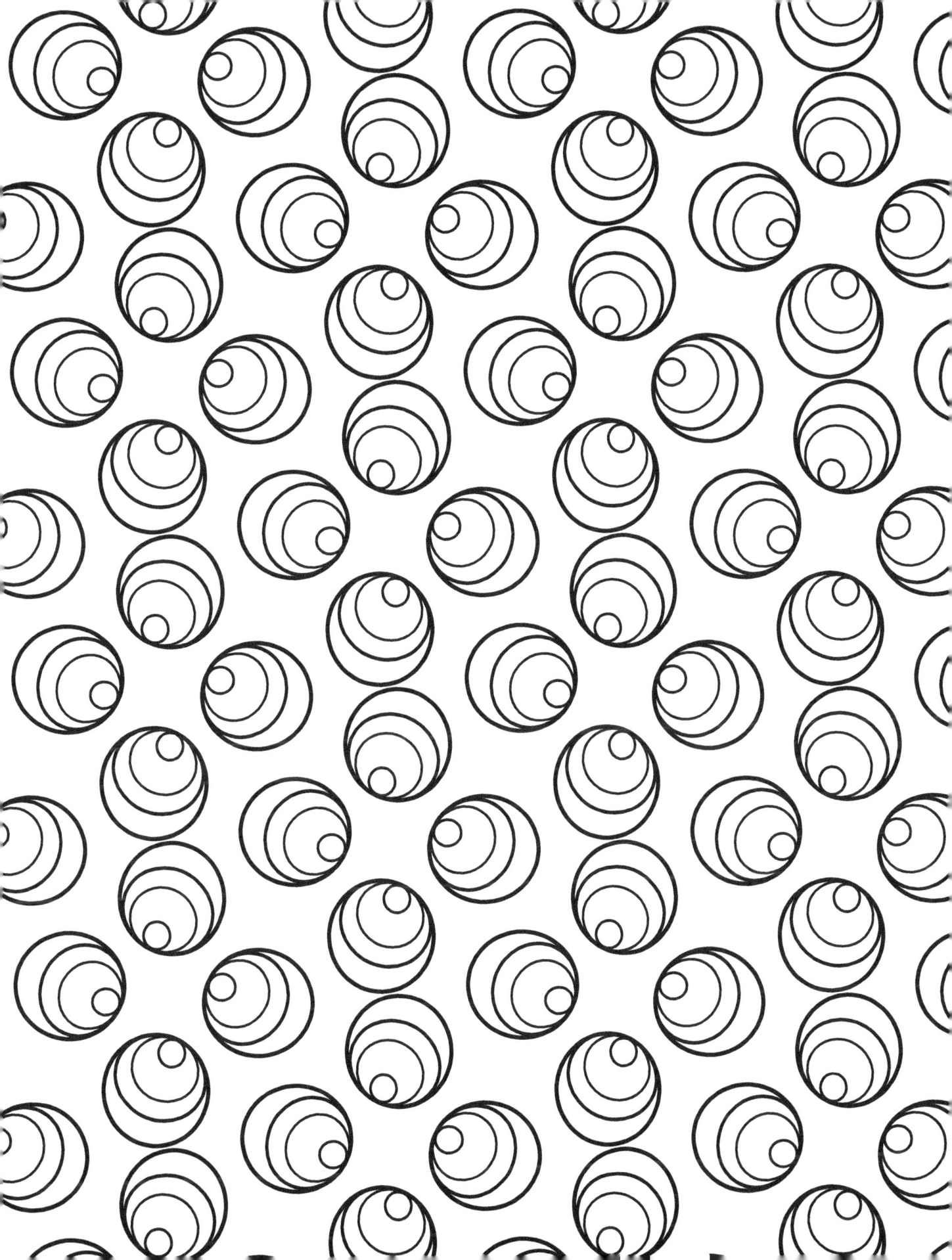

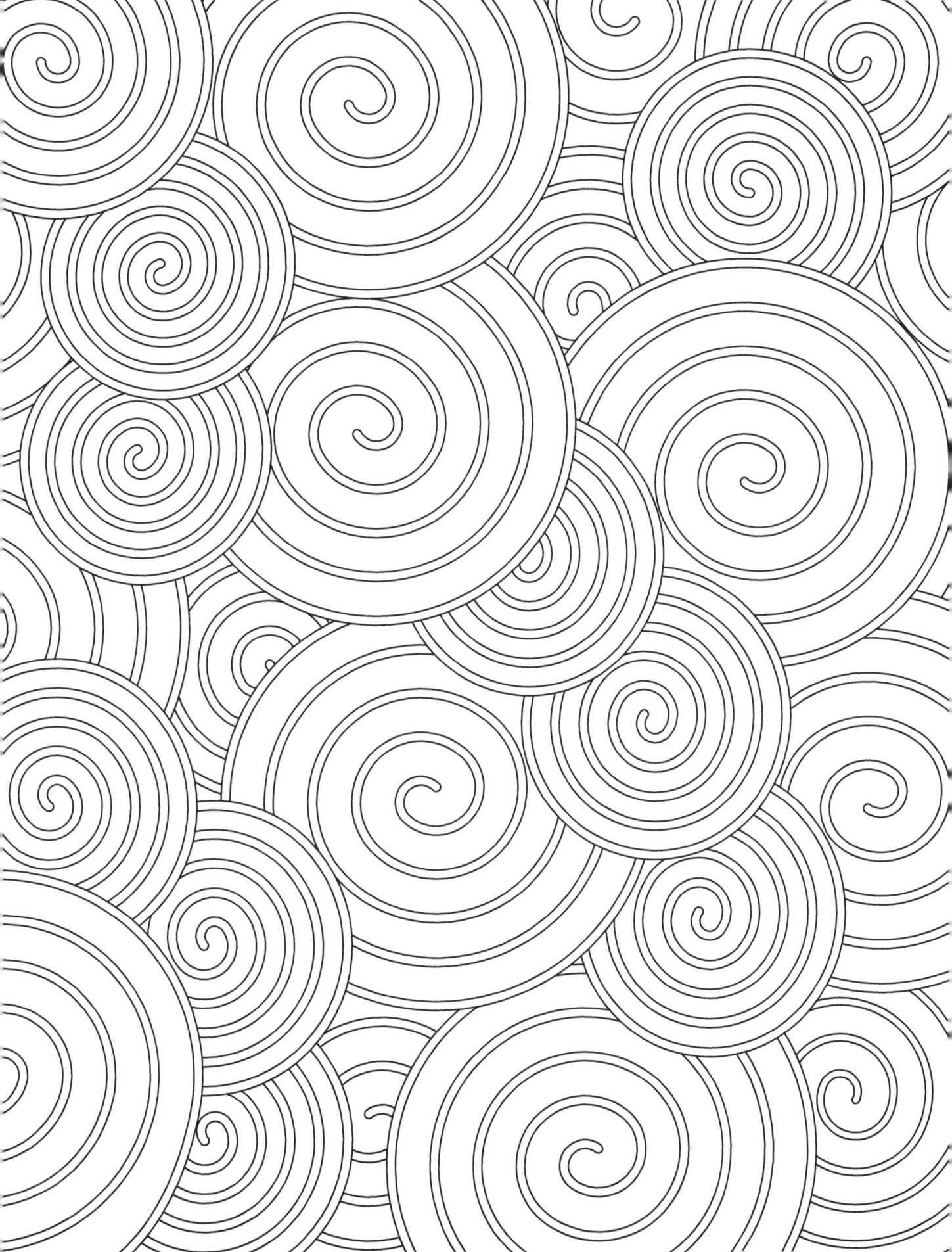

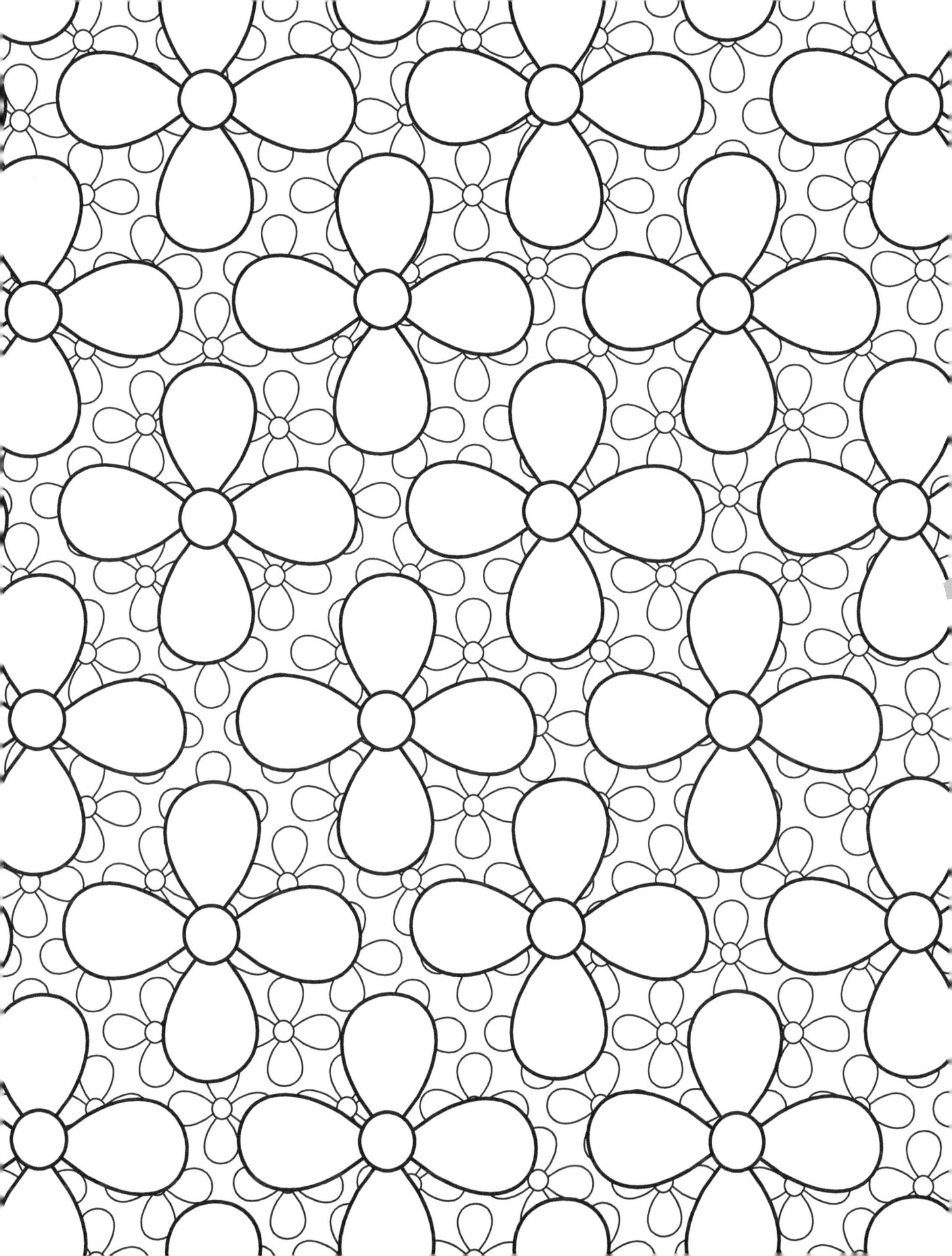

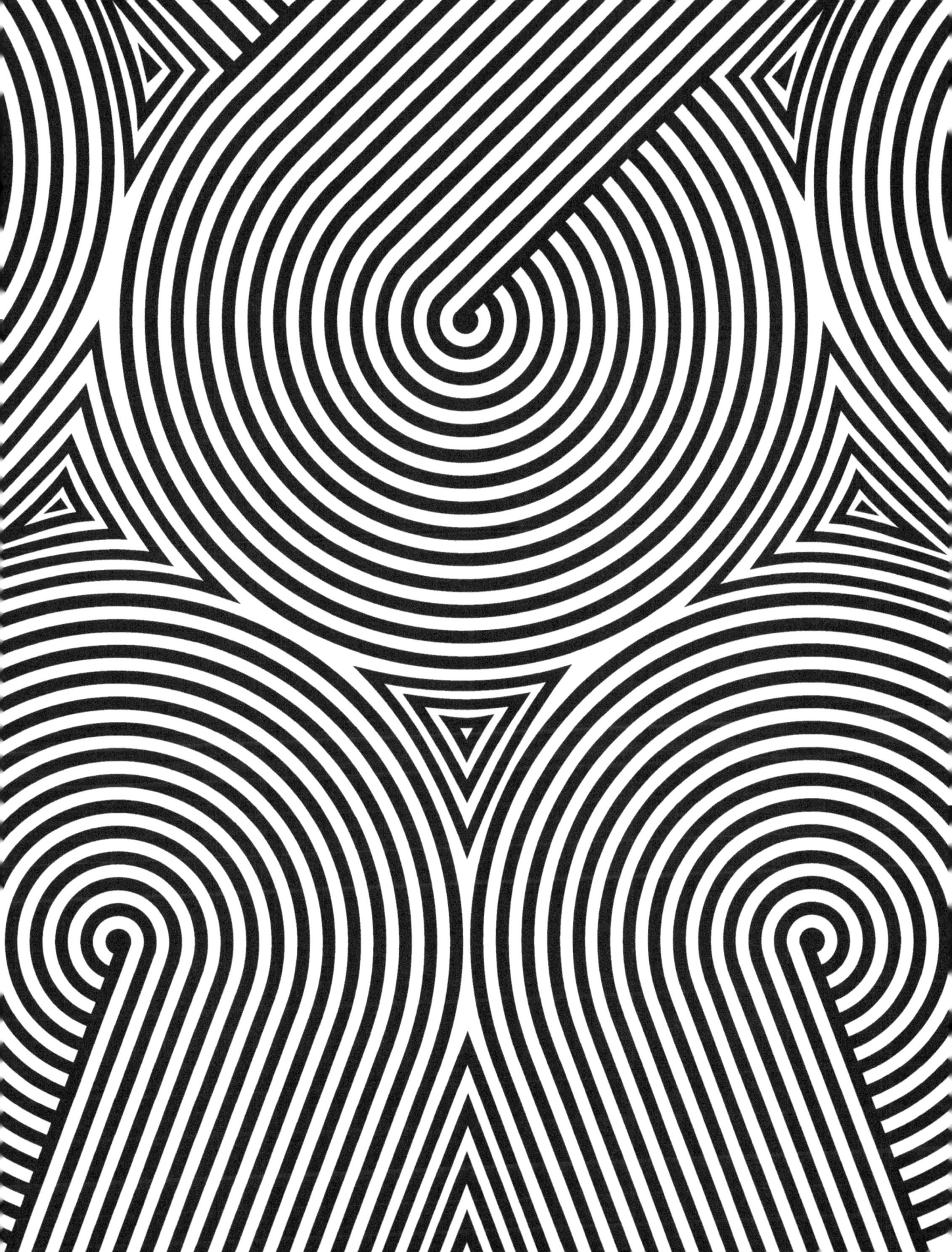

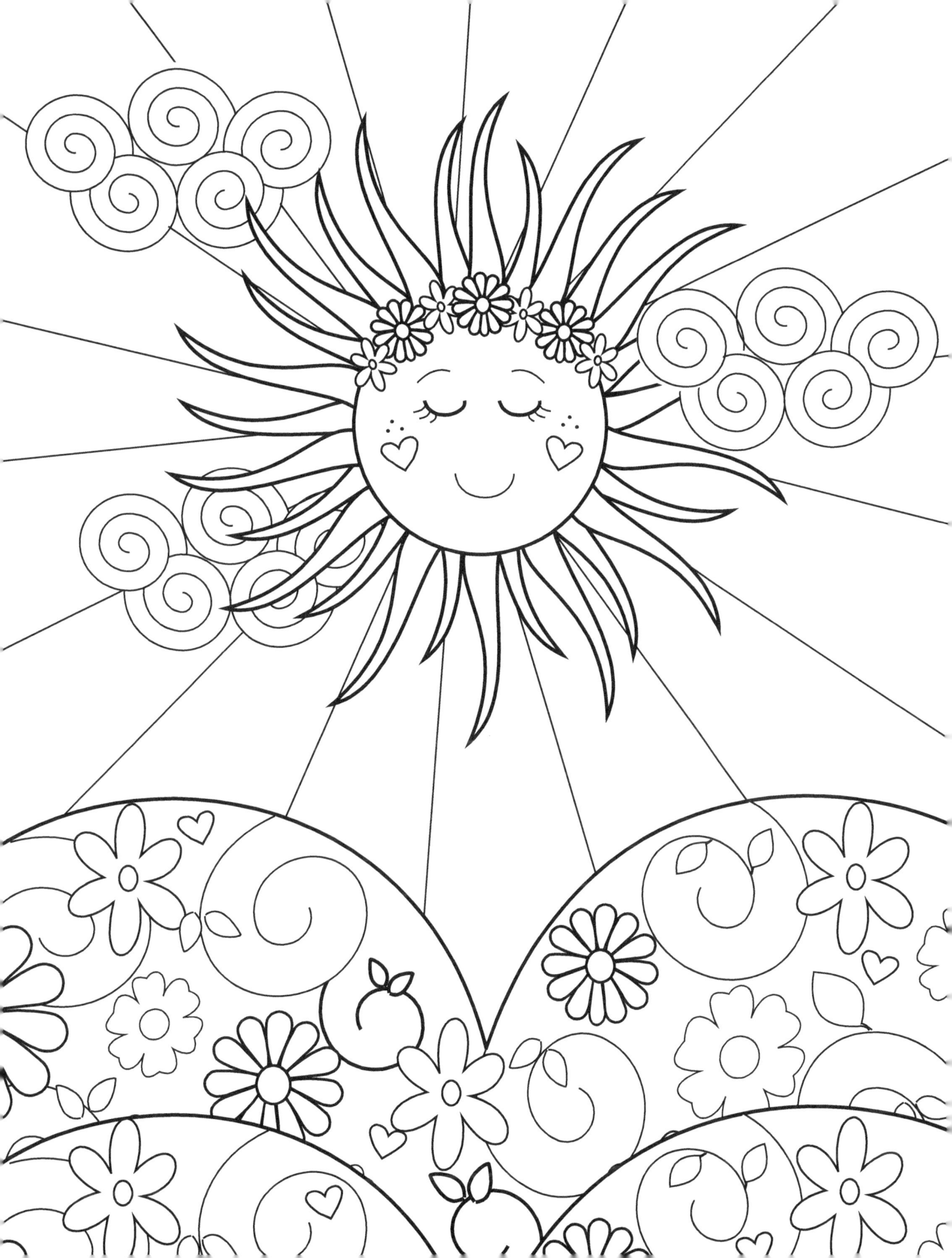

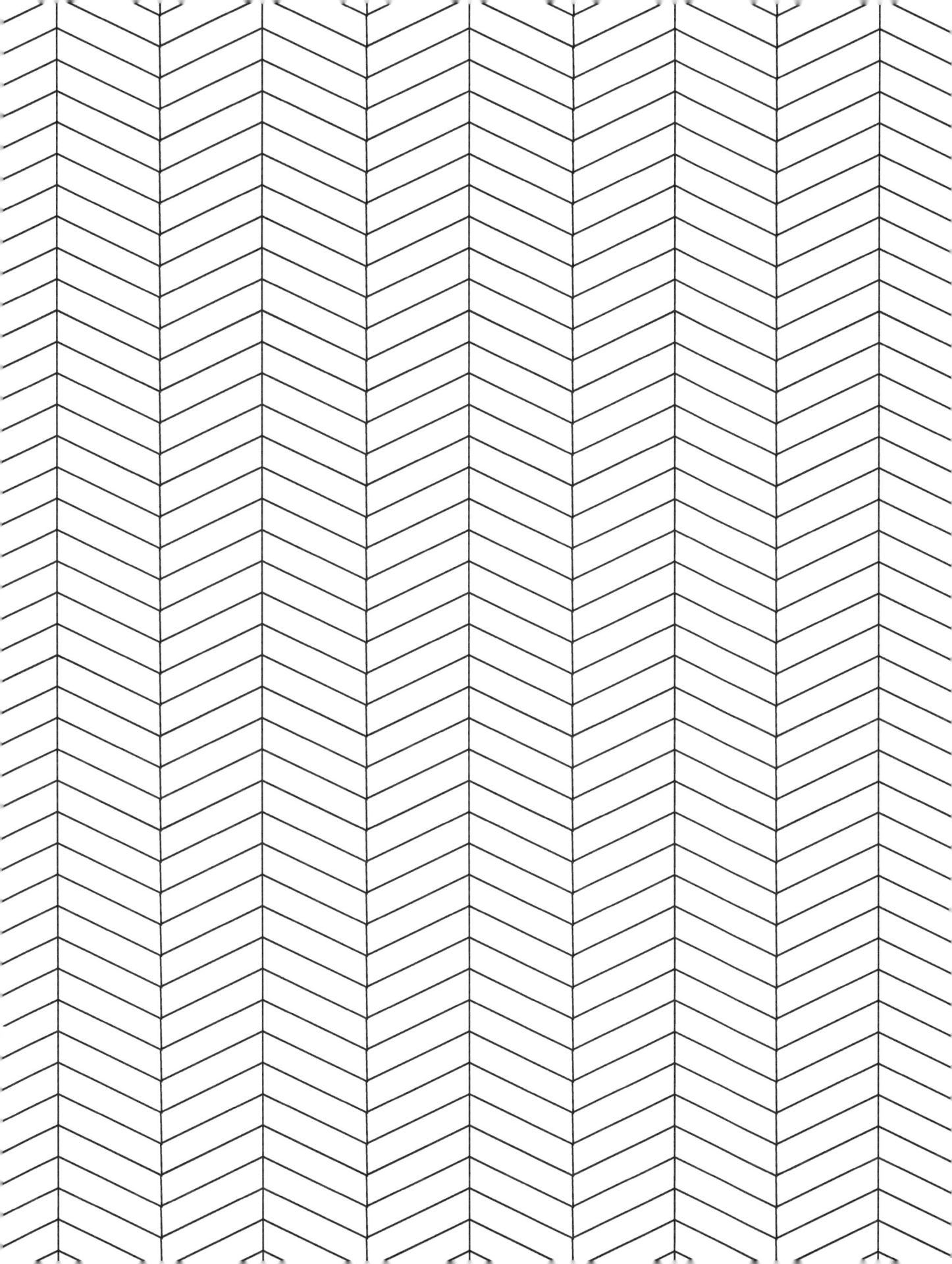

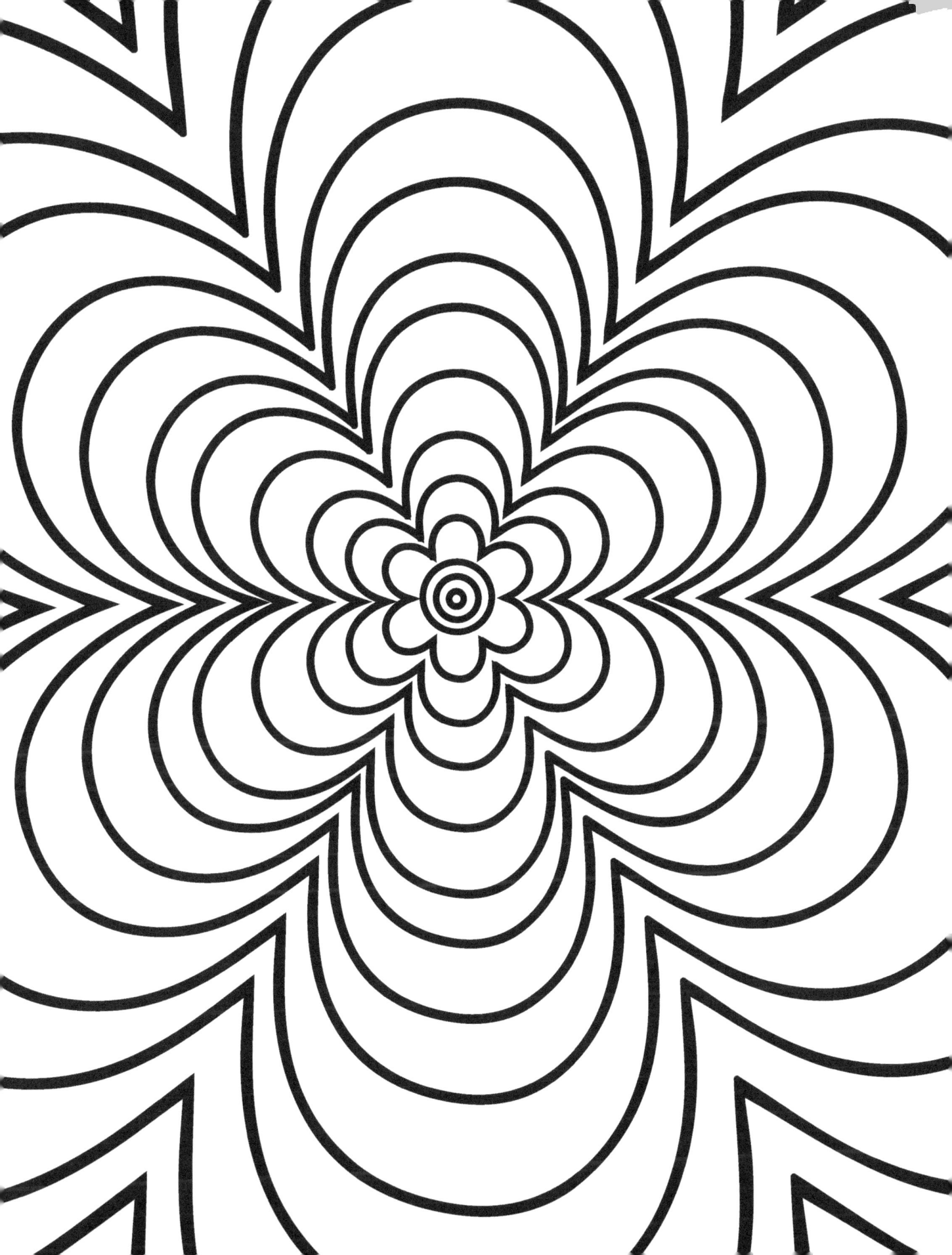

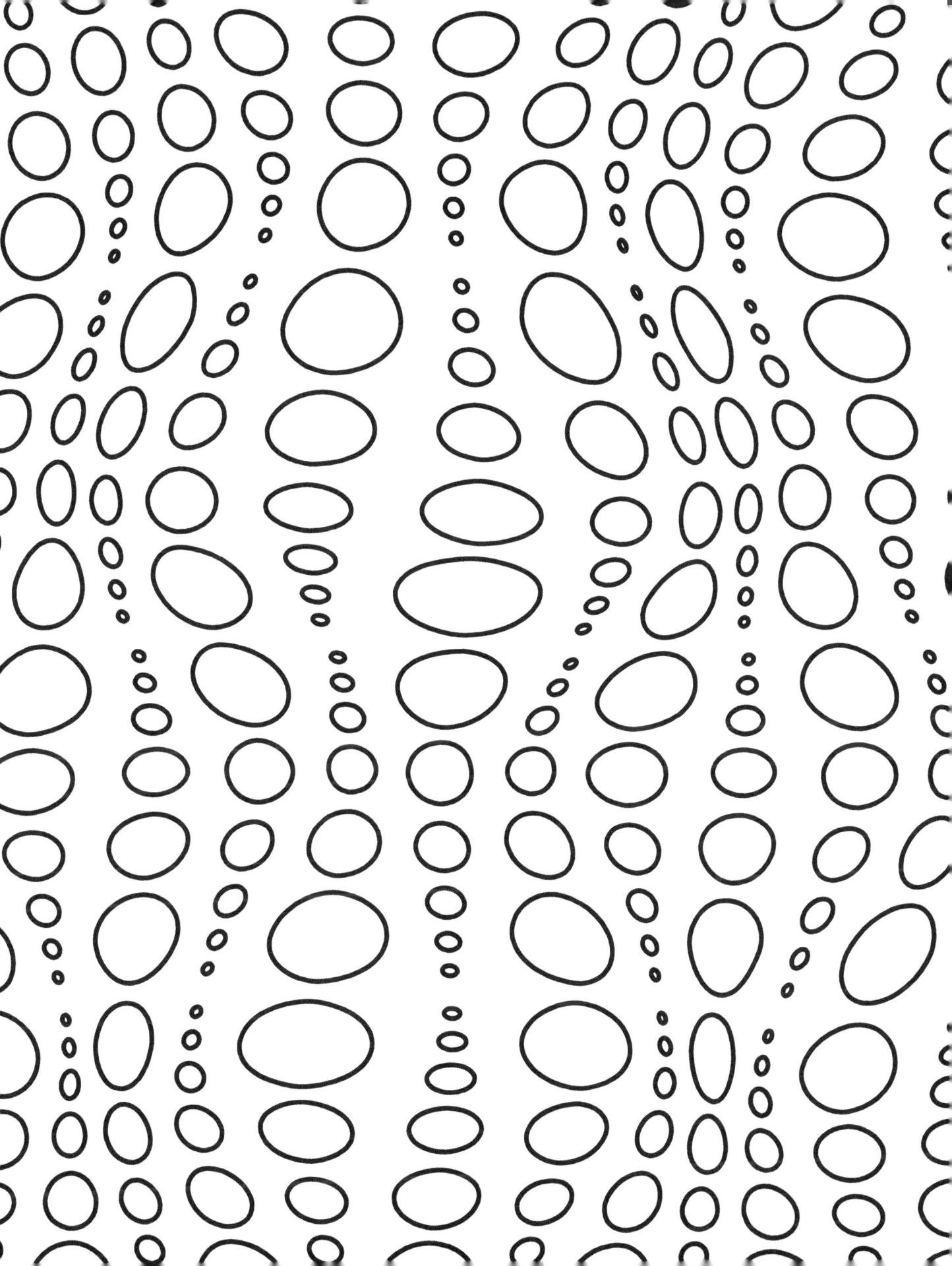

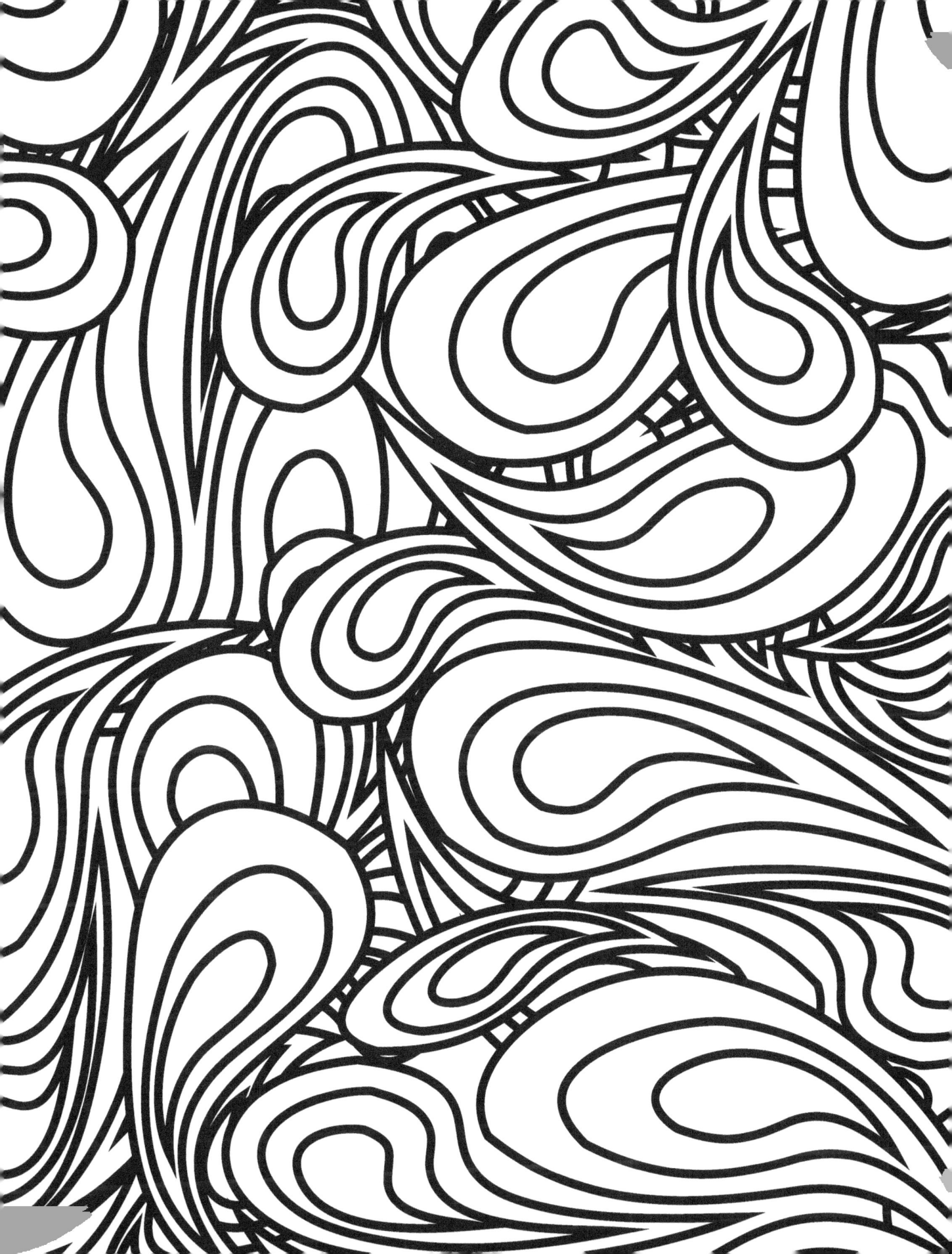

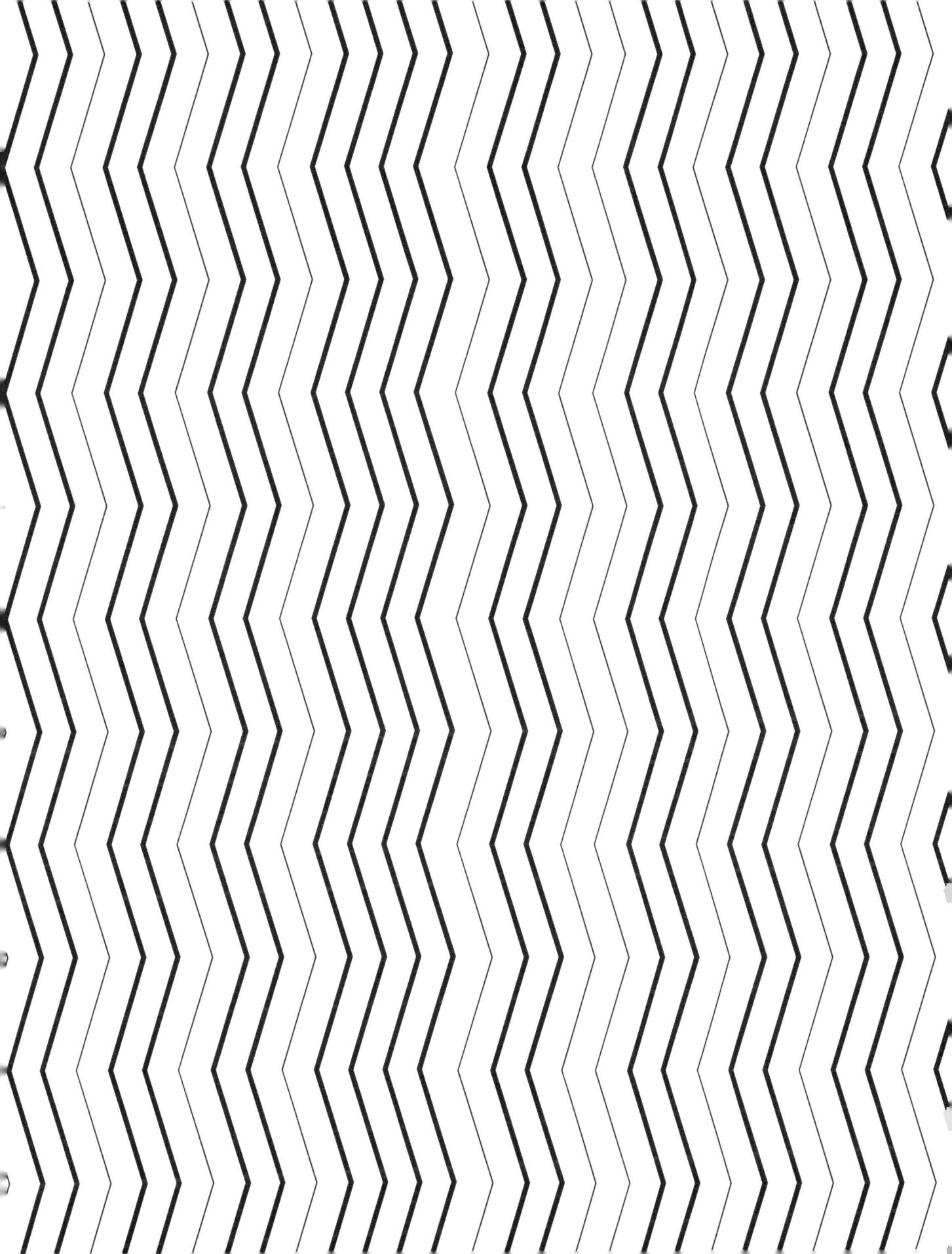

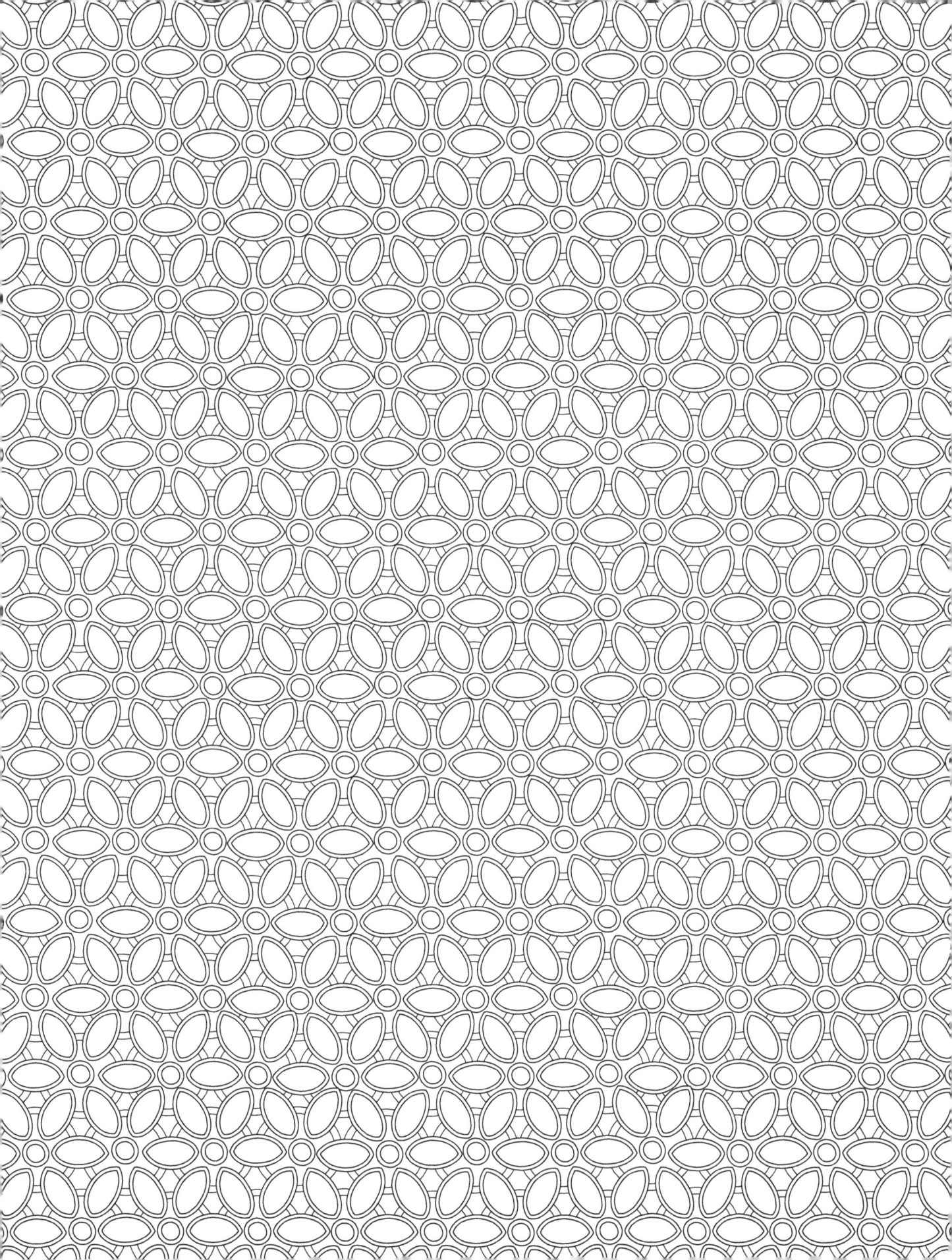

Milkshakes 25¢

Vanilla

Chocolate

Strawberry!

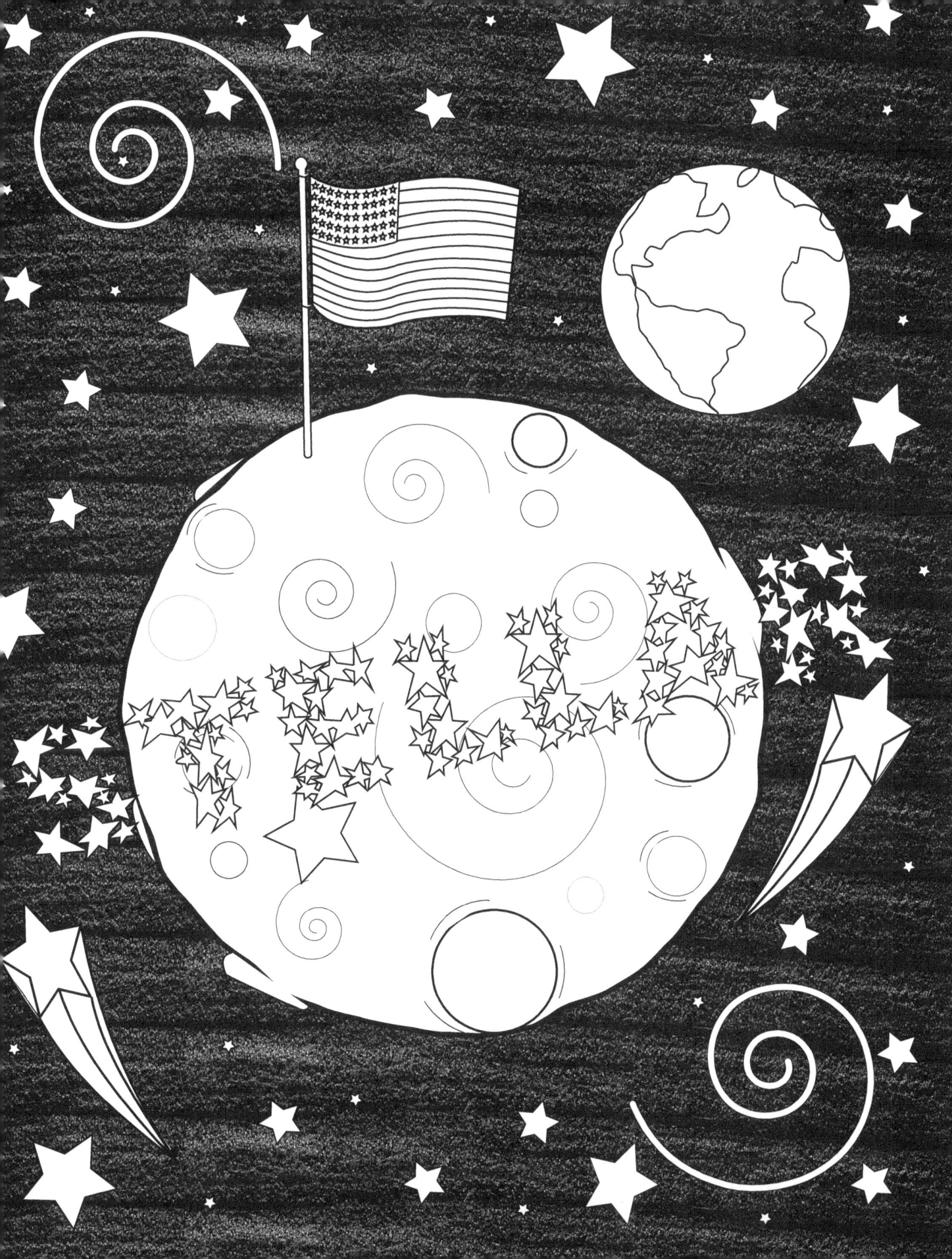

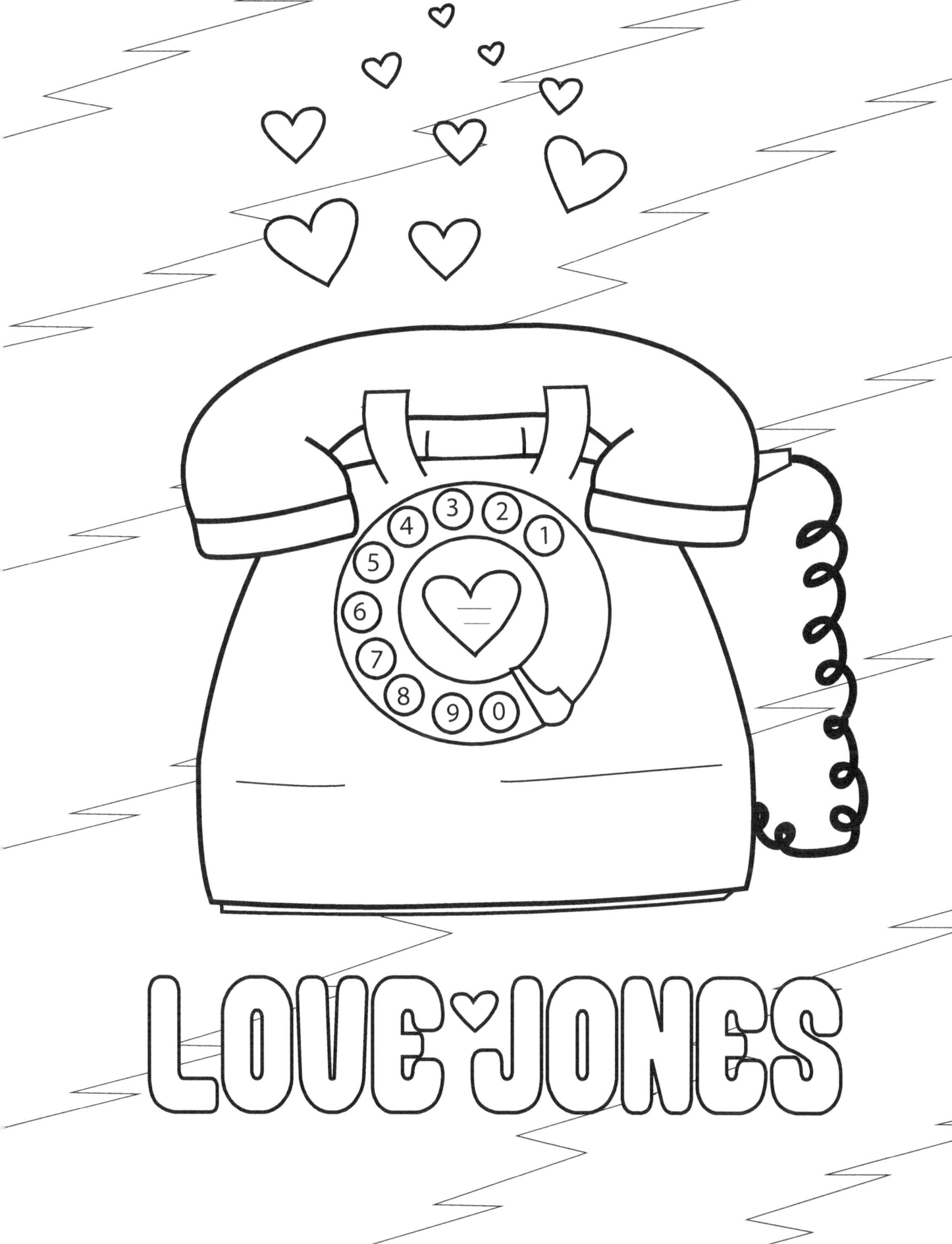

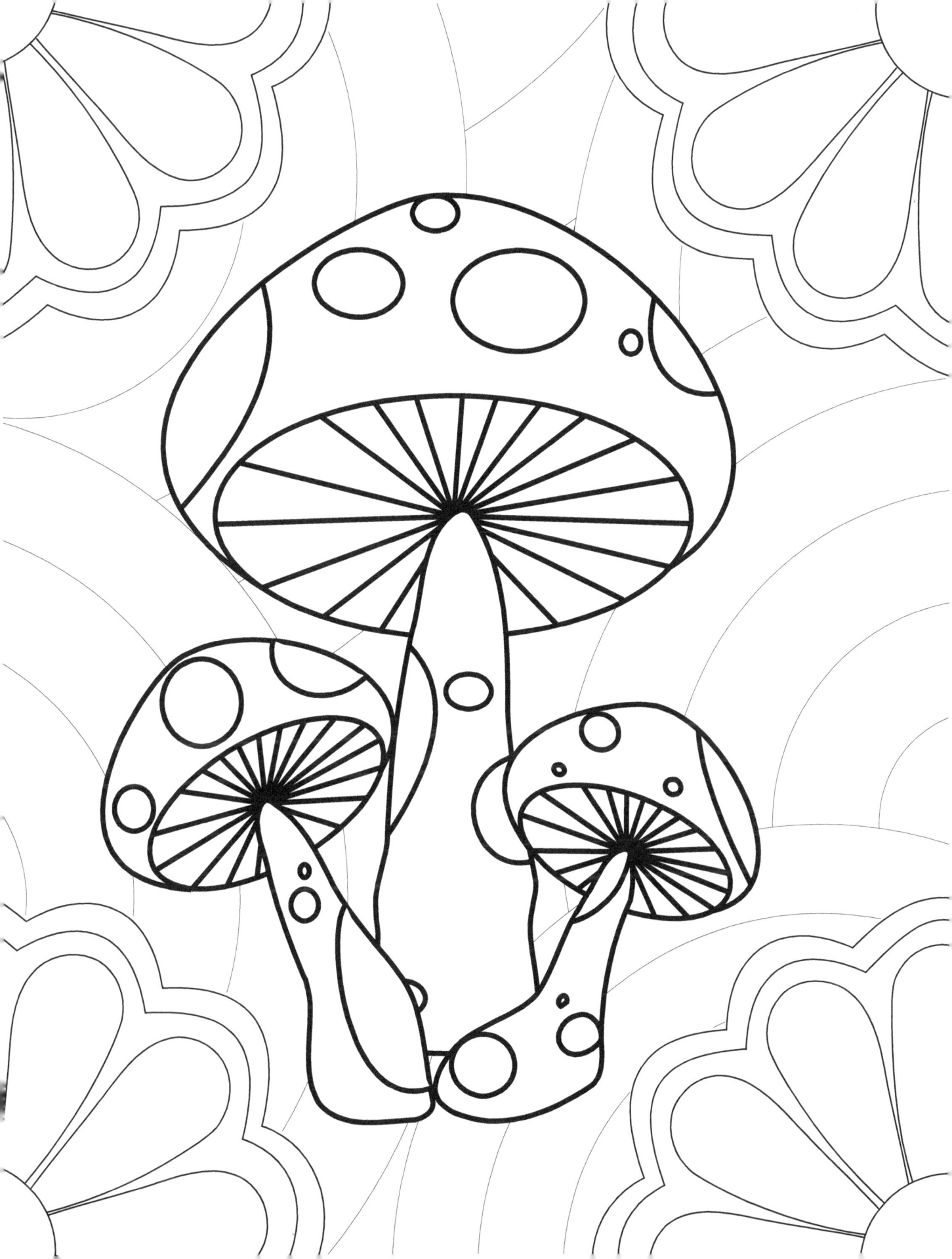

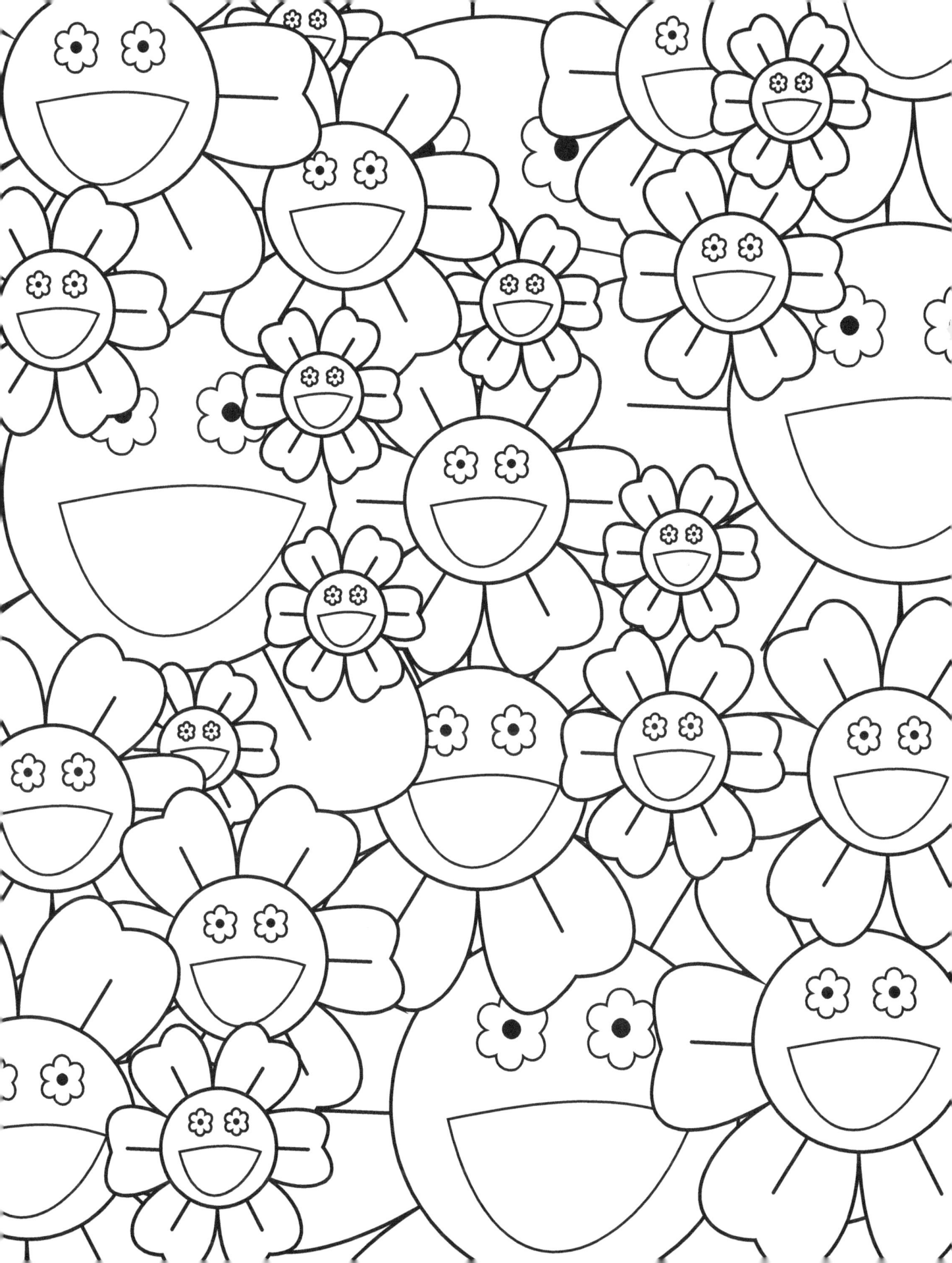

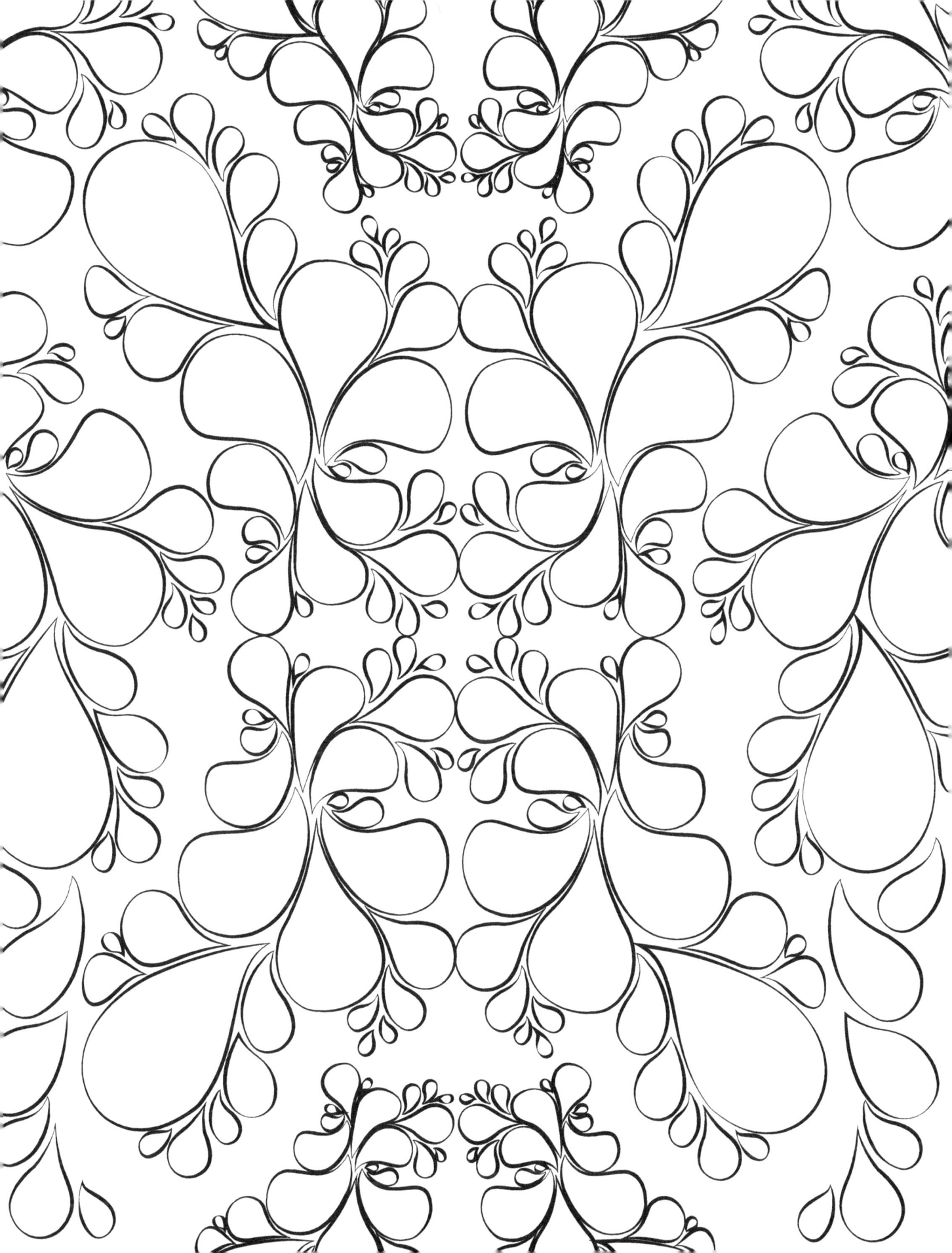

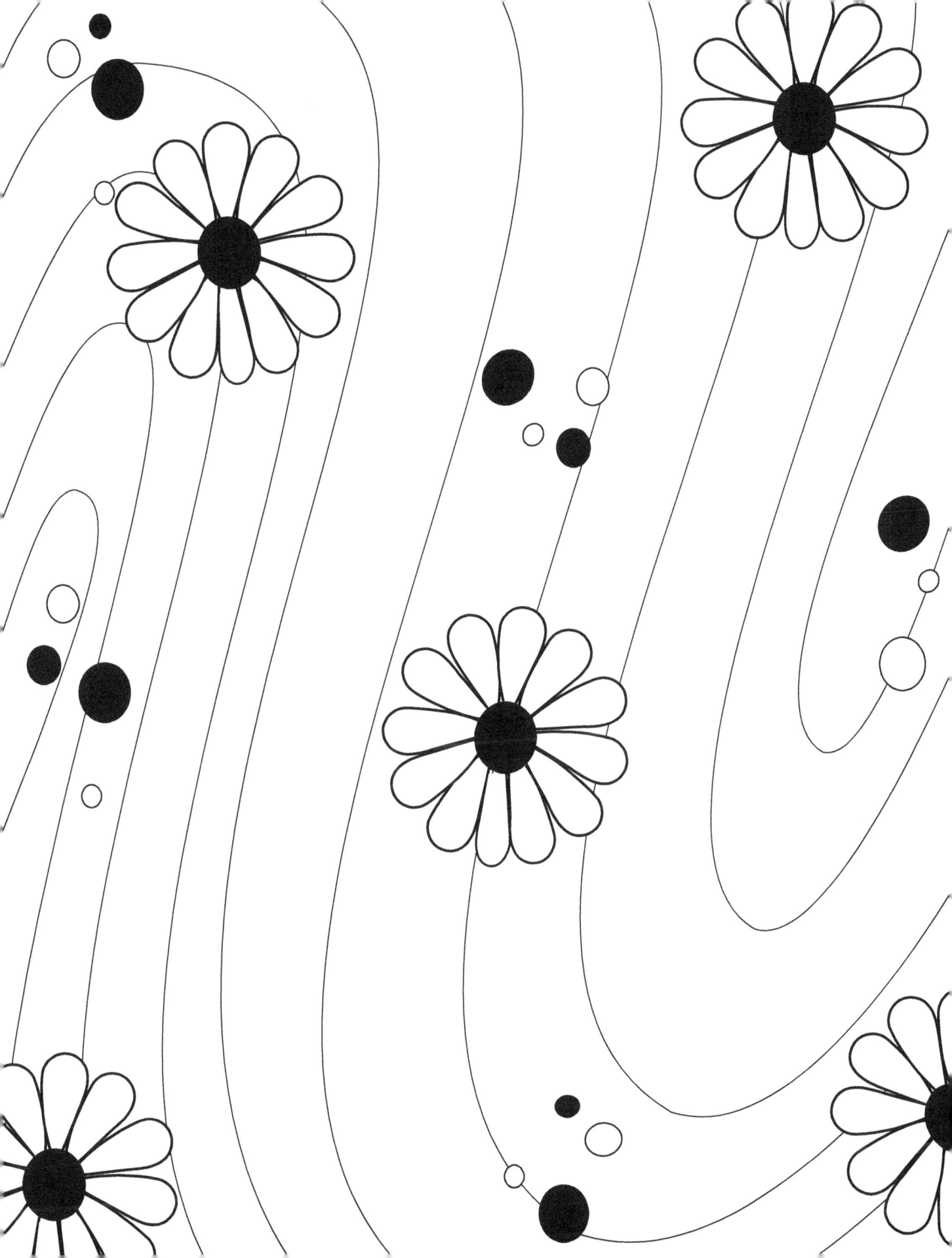

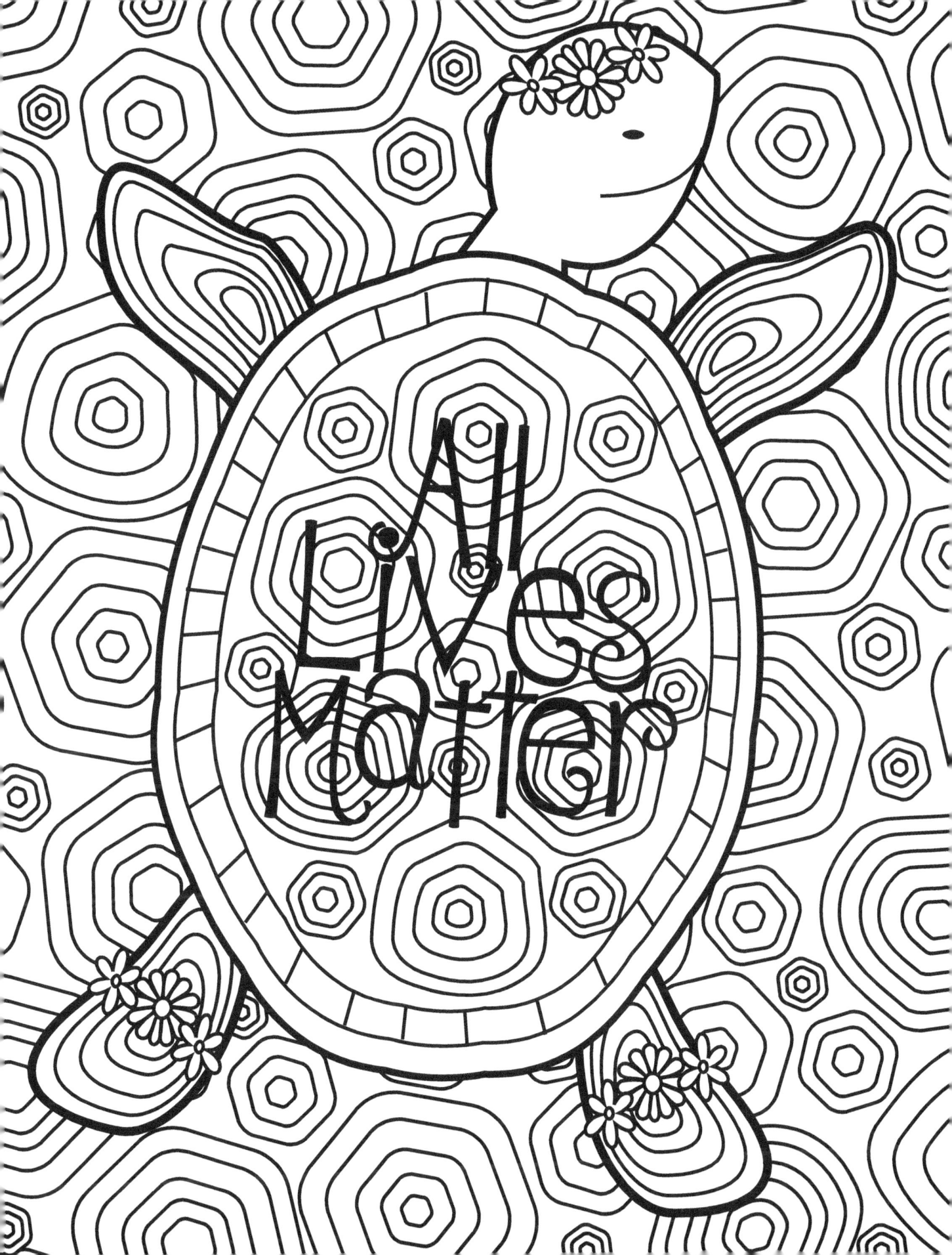

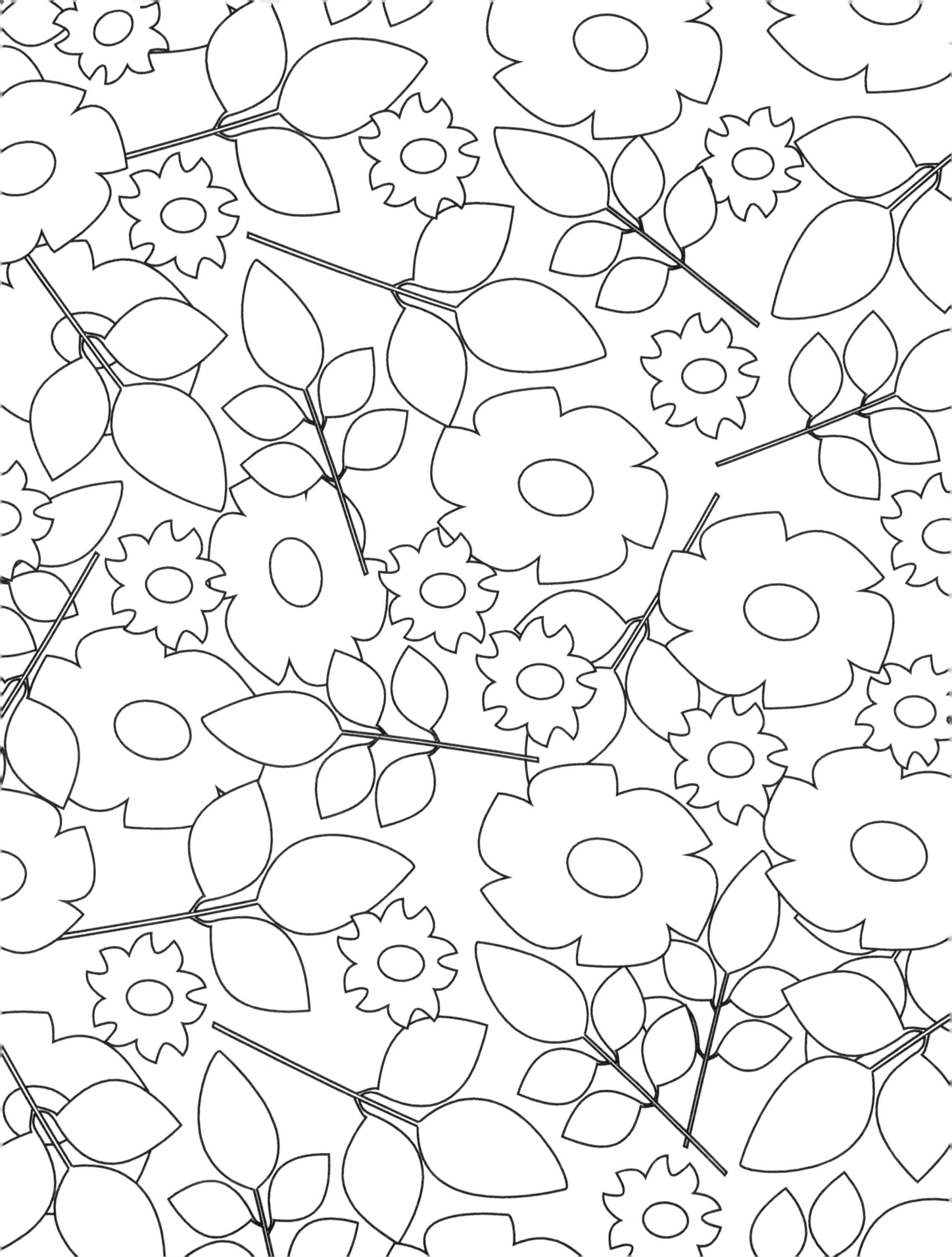

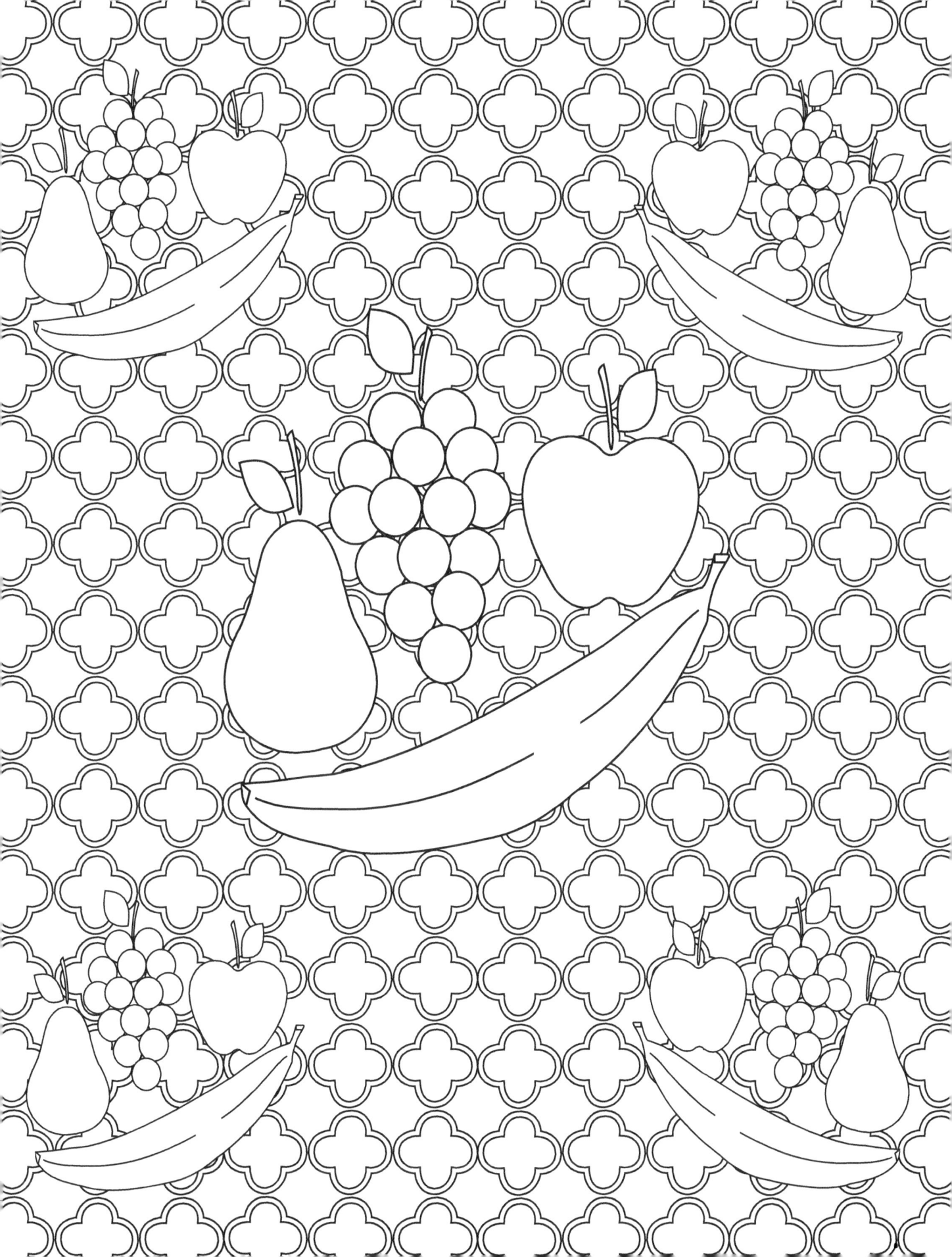

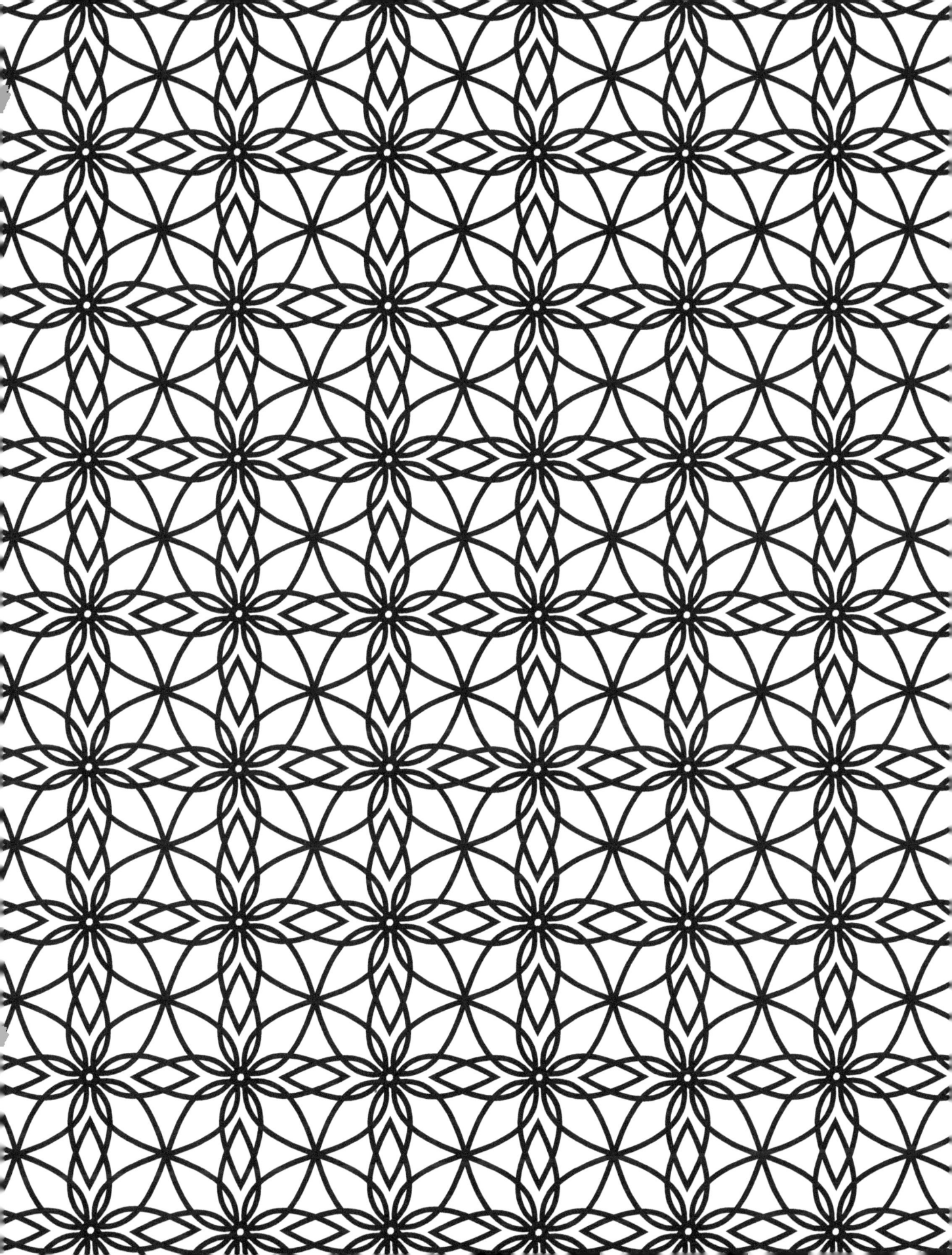

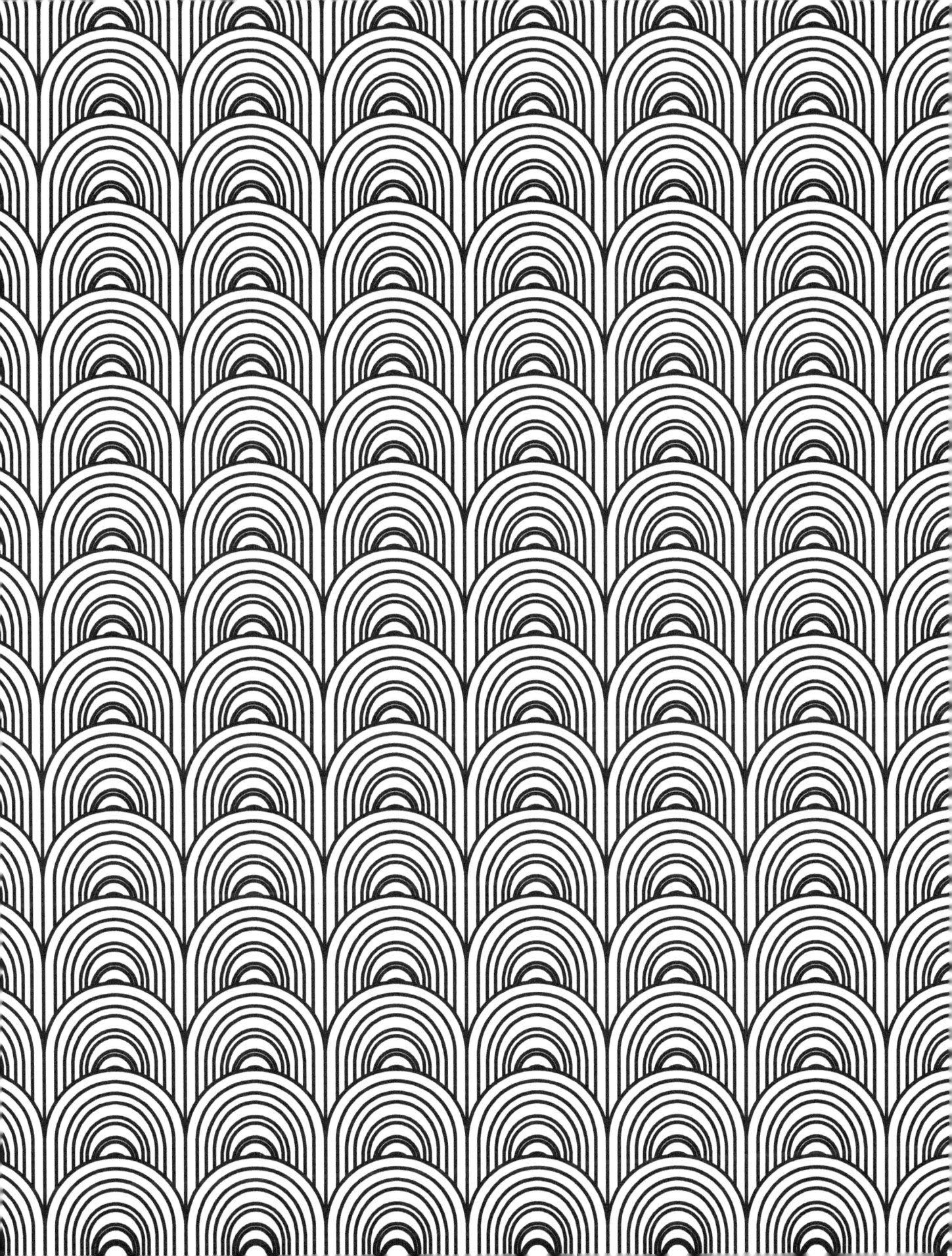

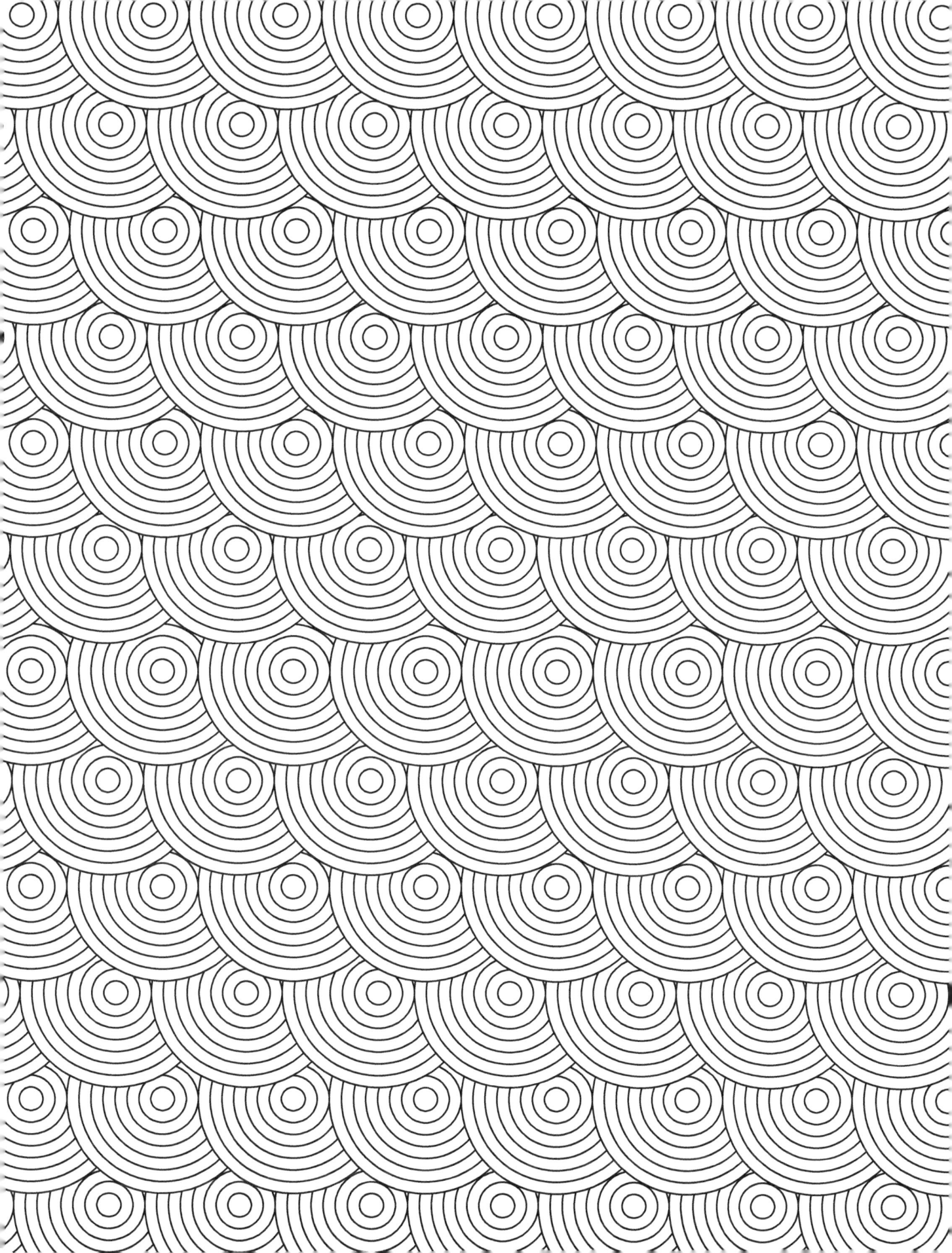

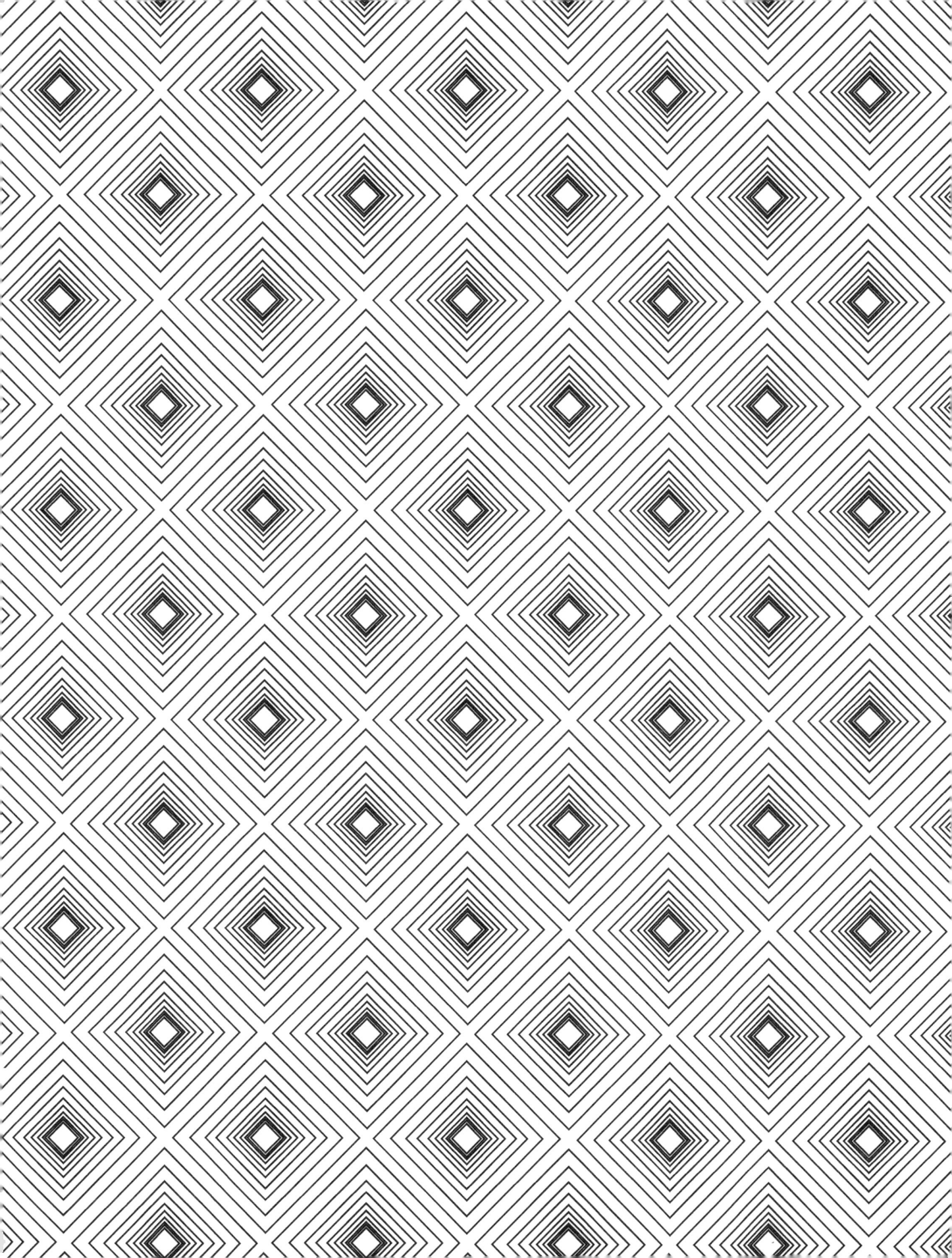

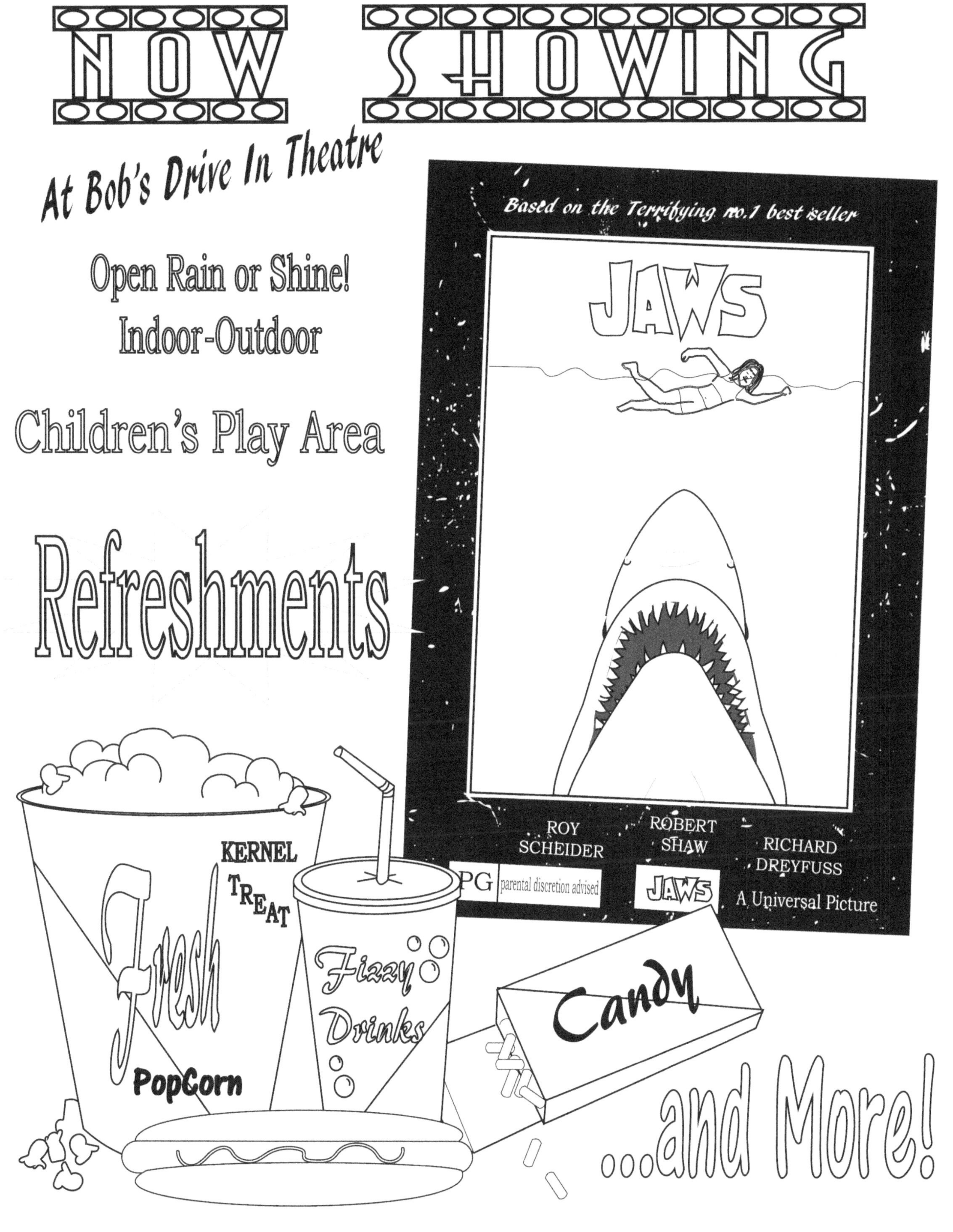

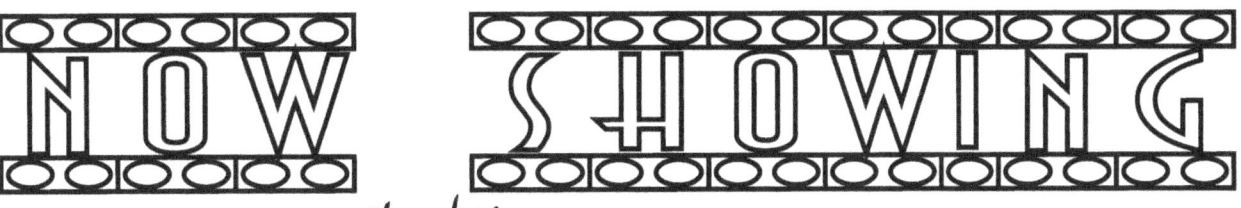

NOW SHOWING

At Bob's Drive In Theatre

Open Rain or Shine!
Indoor-Outdoor

Children's Play Area

Refreshments

KERNEL TREAT

Fresh

PopCorn

Fizzy Drinks

Candy

...and More!

Based on the Terrifying no.1 best seller

JAWS

ROY SCHEIDER   ROBERT SHAW   RICHARD DREYFUSS

PG | parental discretion advised   JAWS   A Universal Picture

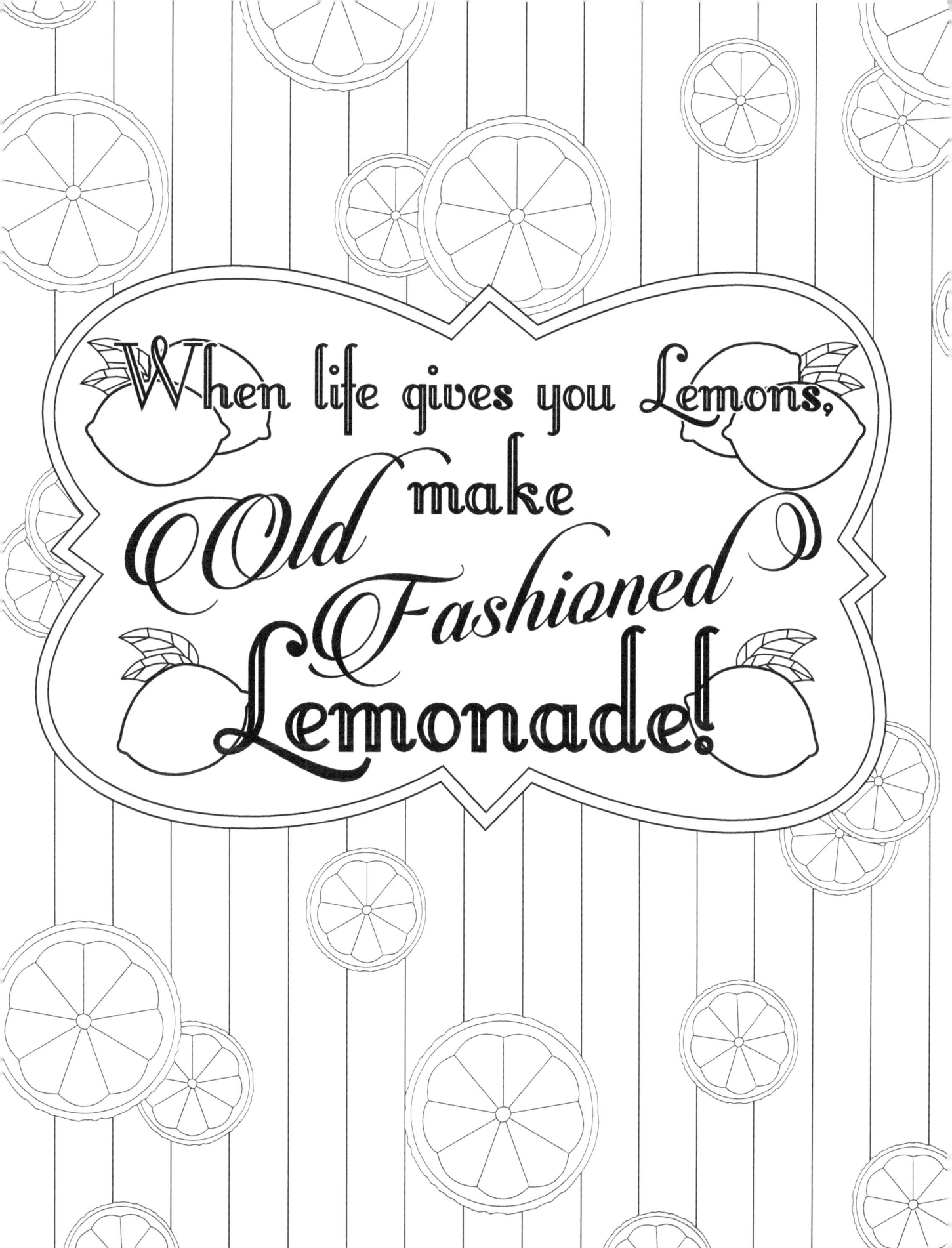

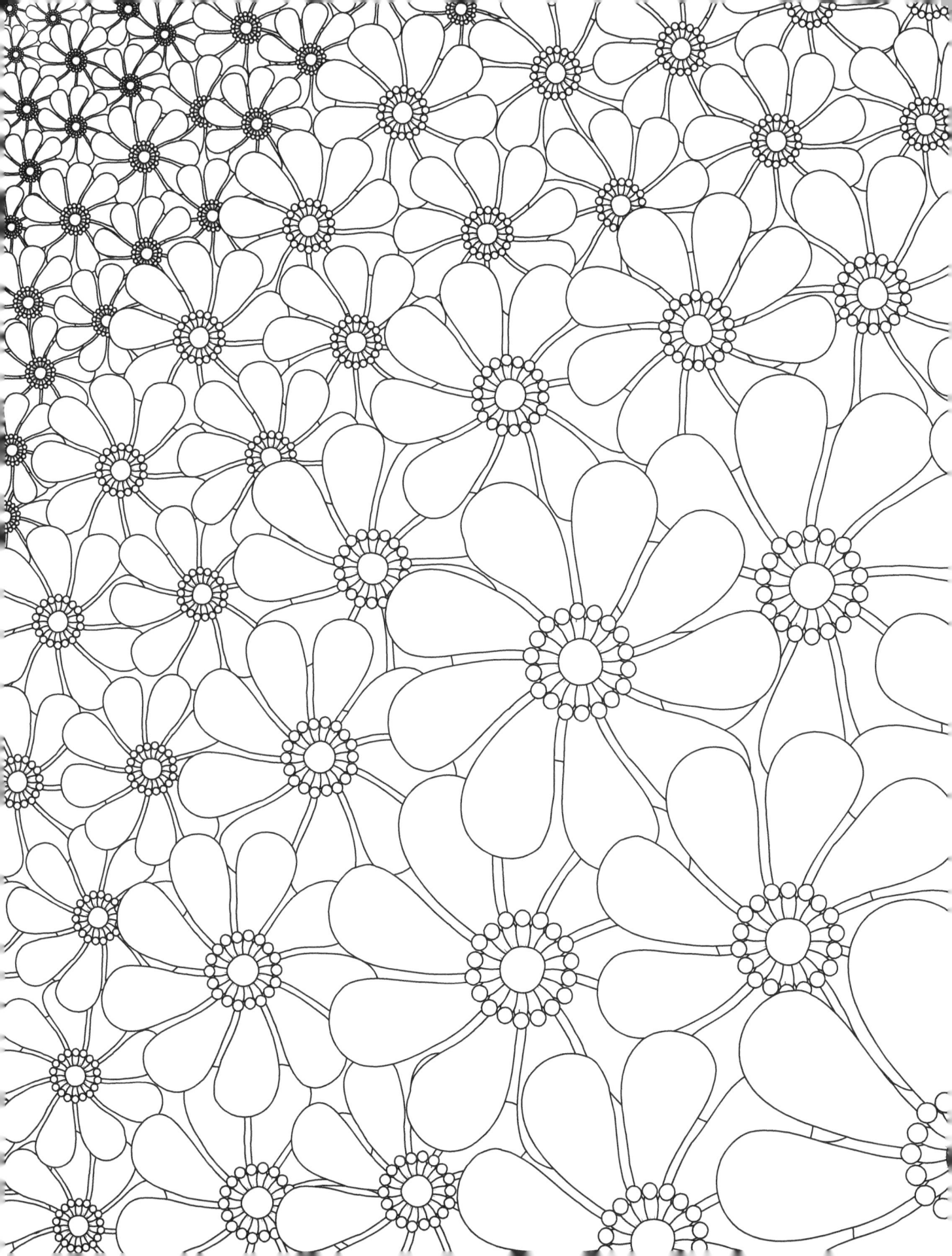

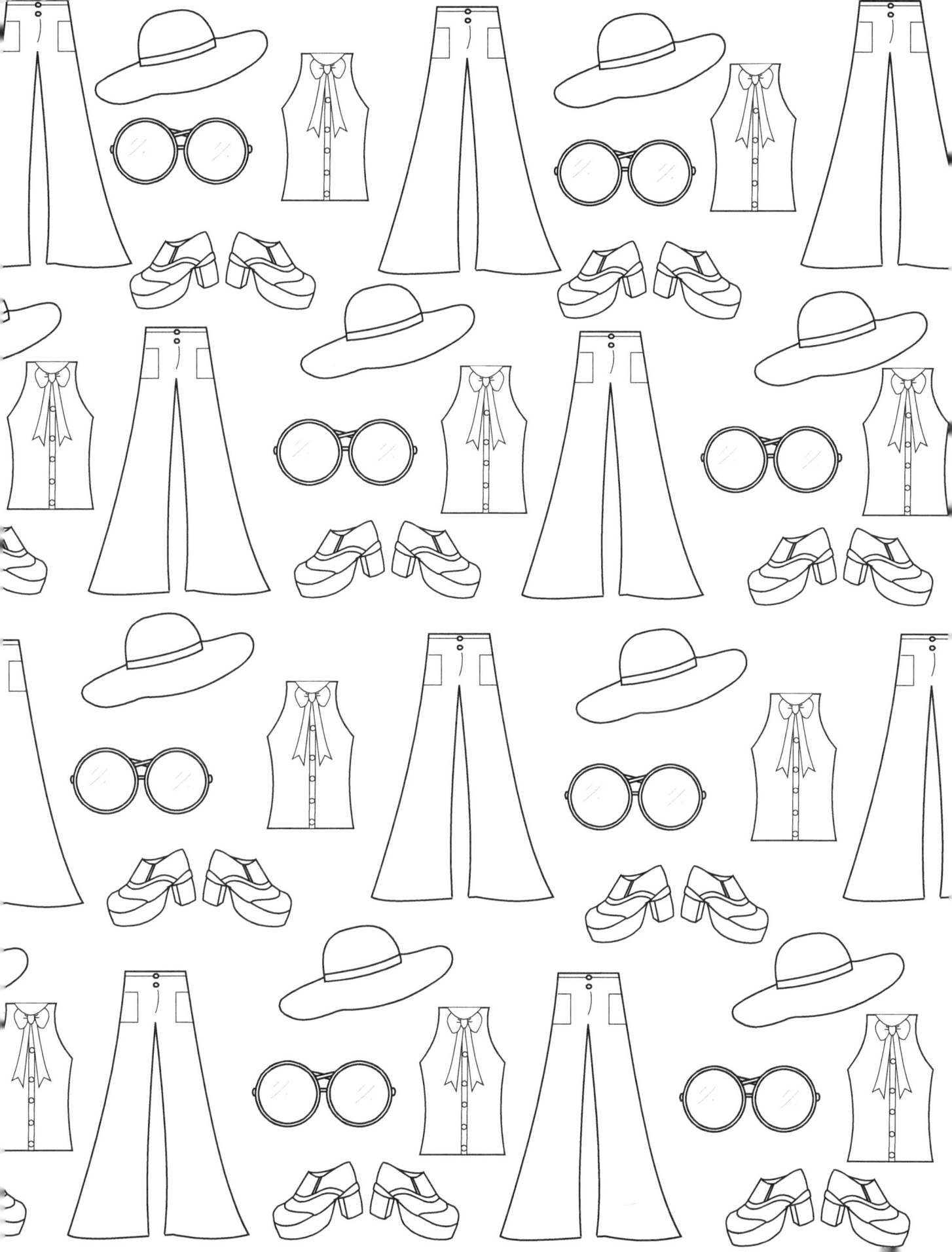

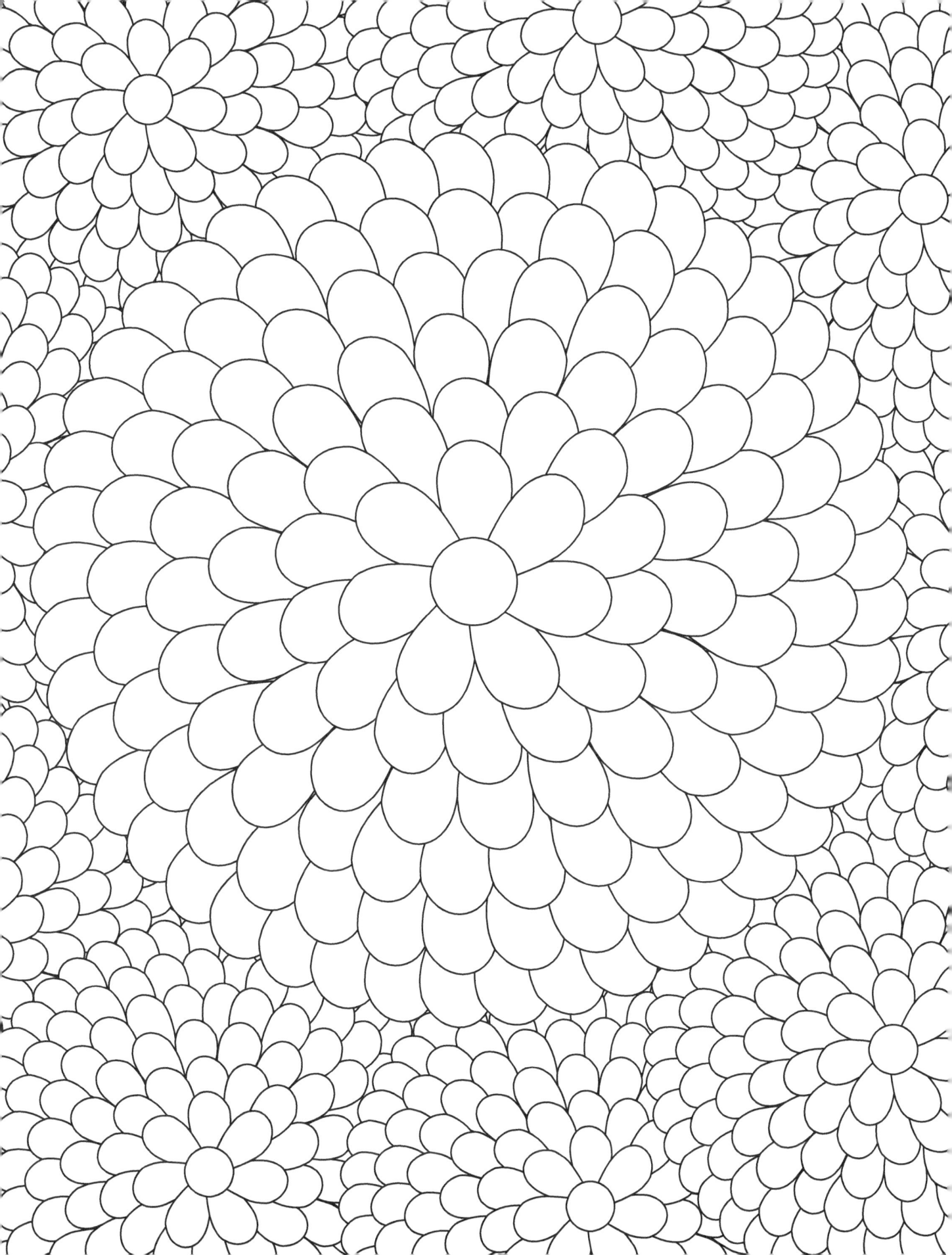

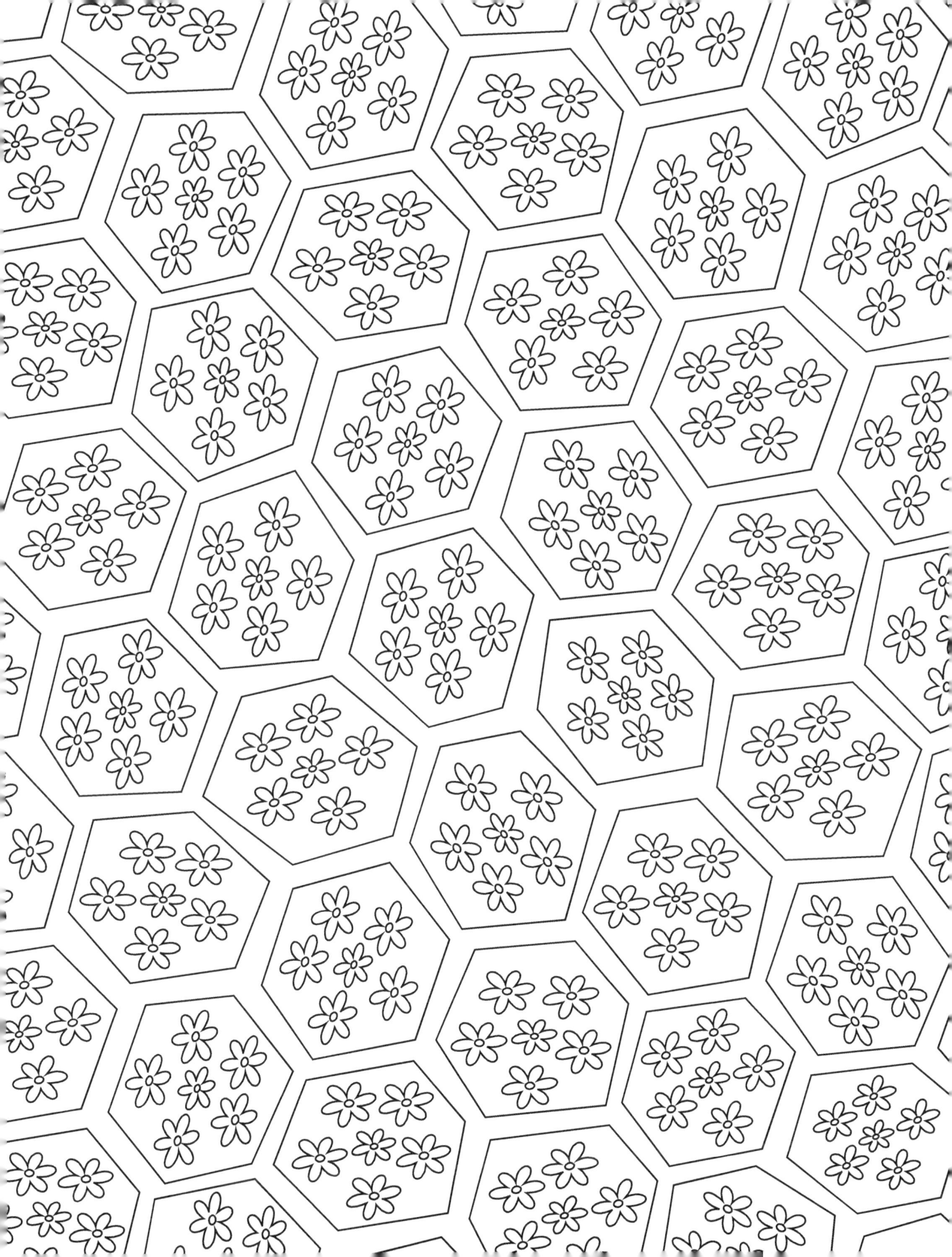

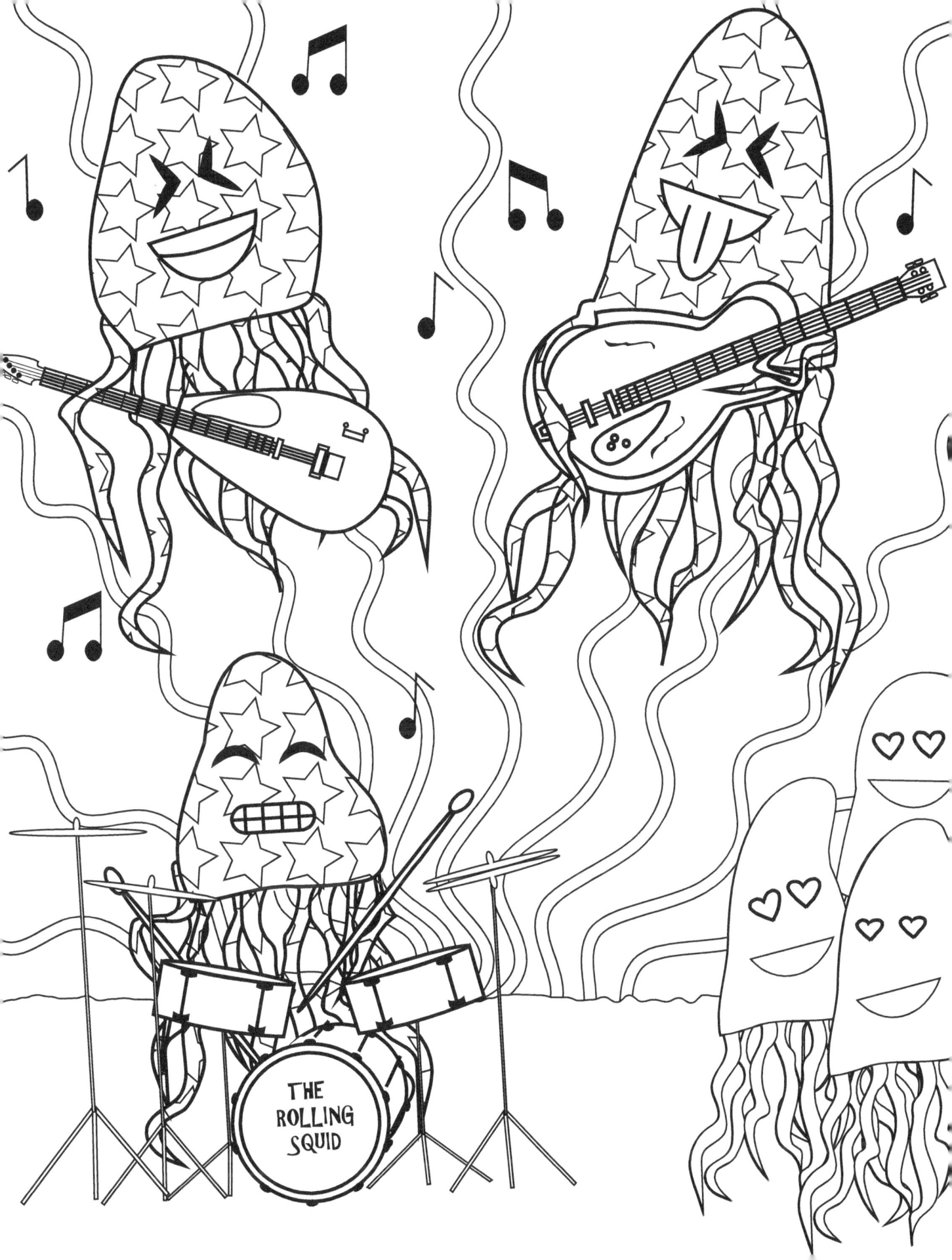

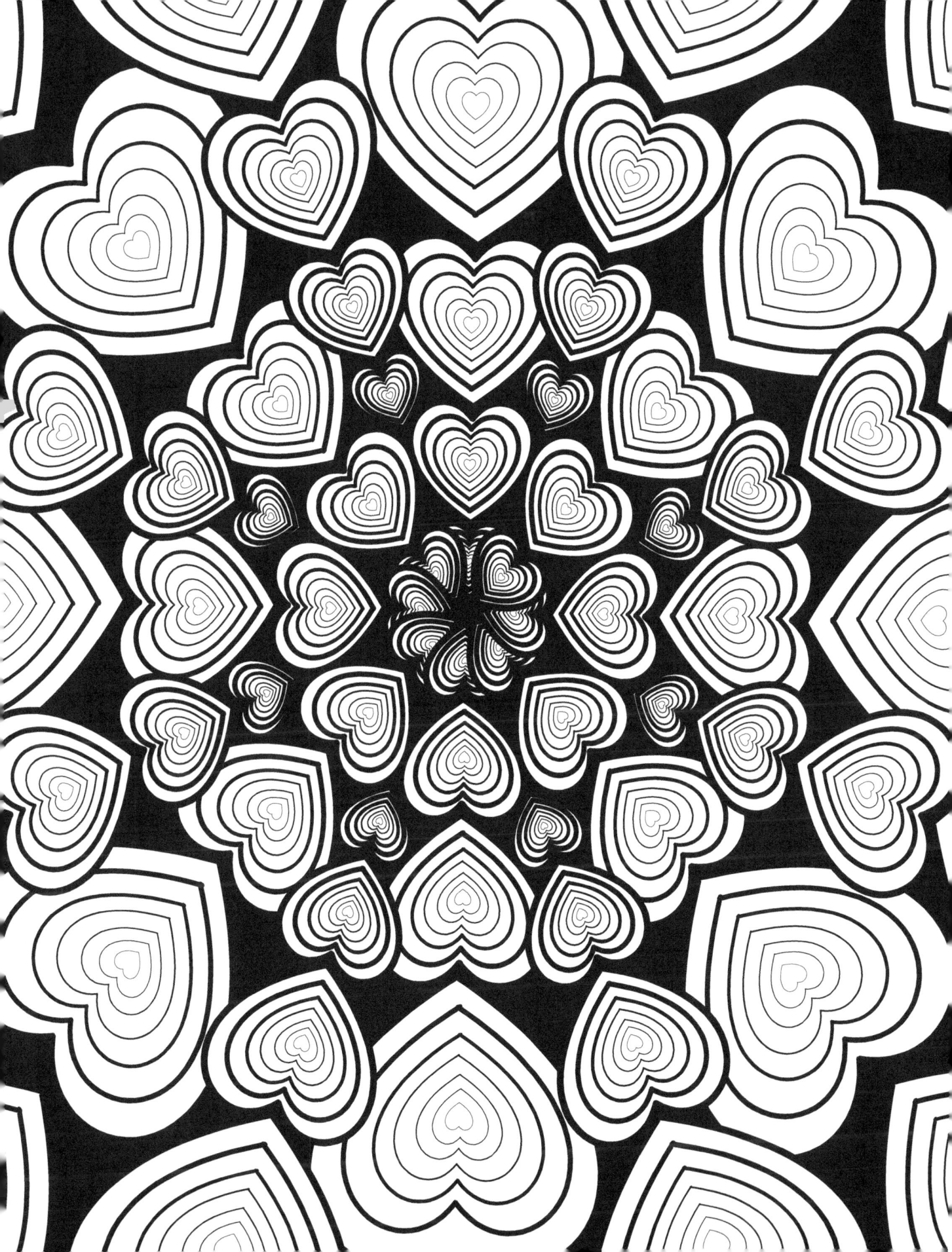

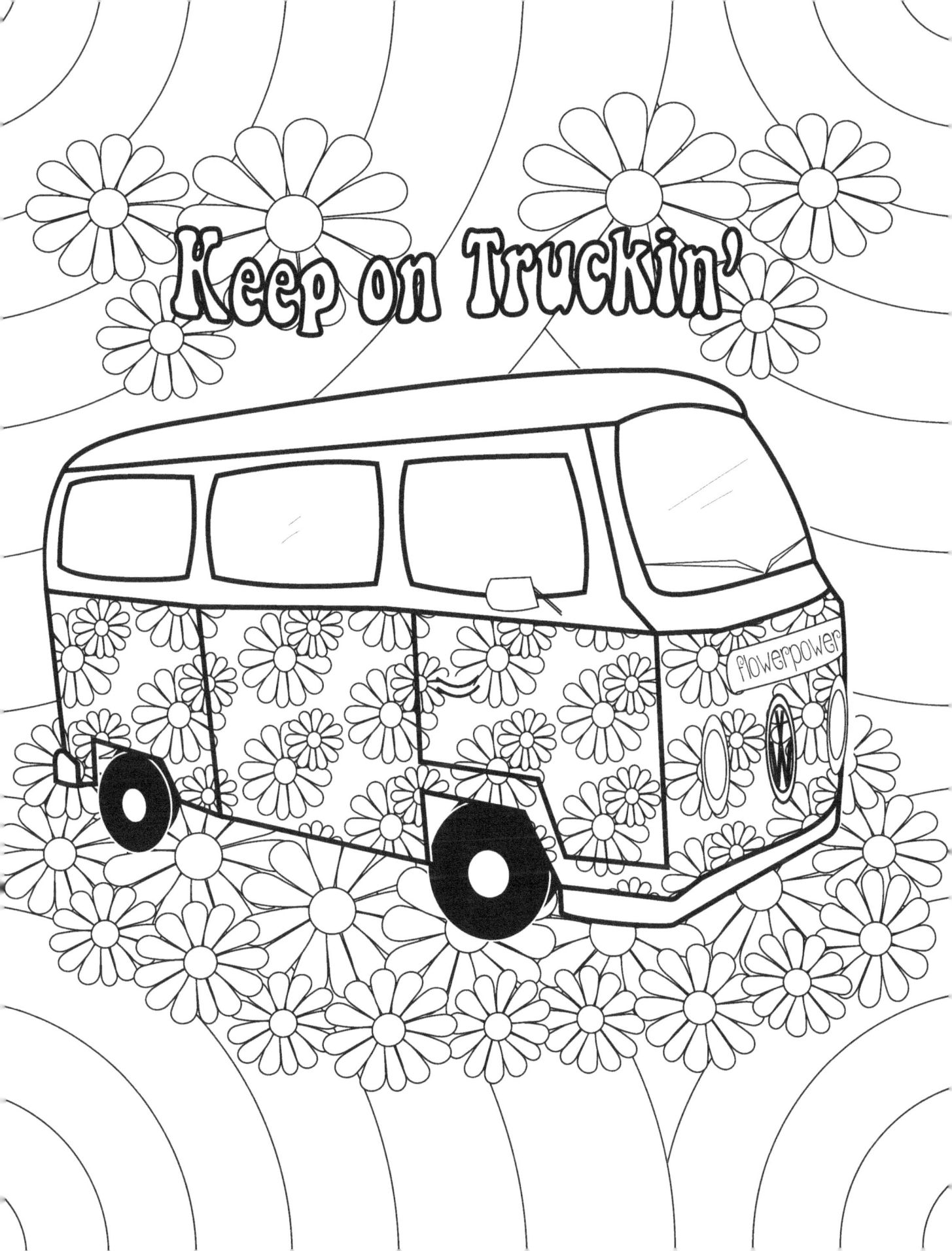

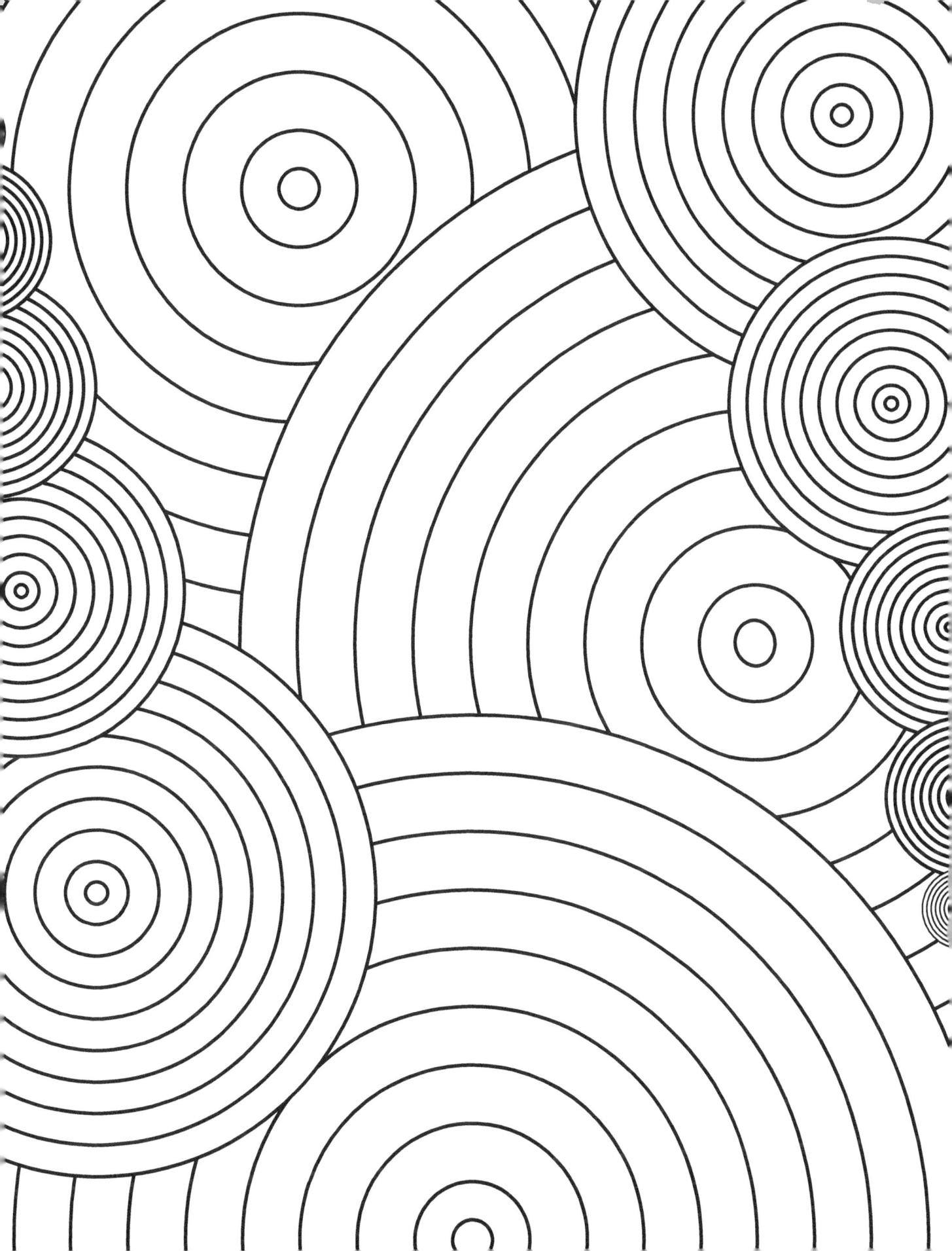

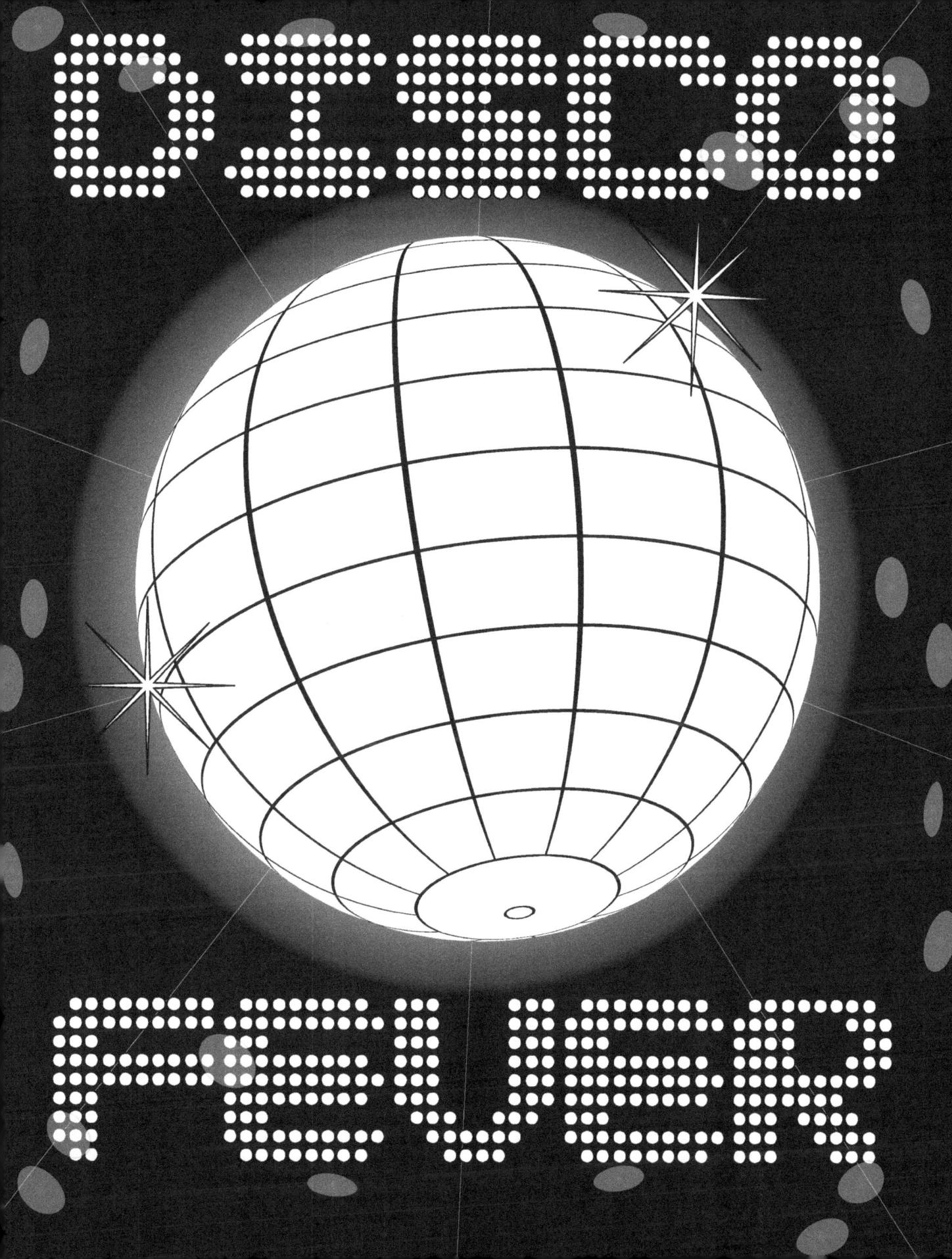

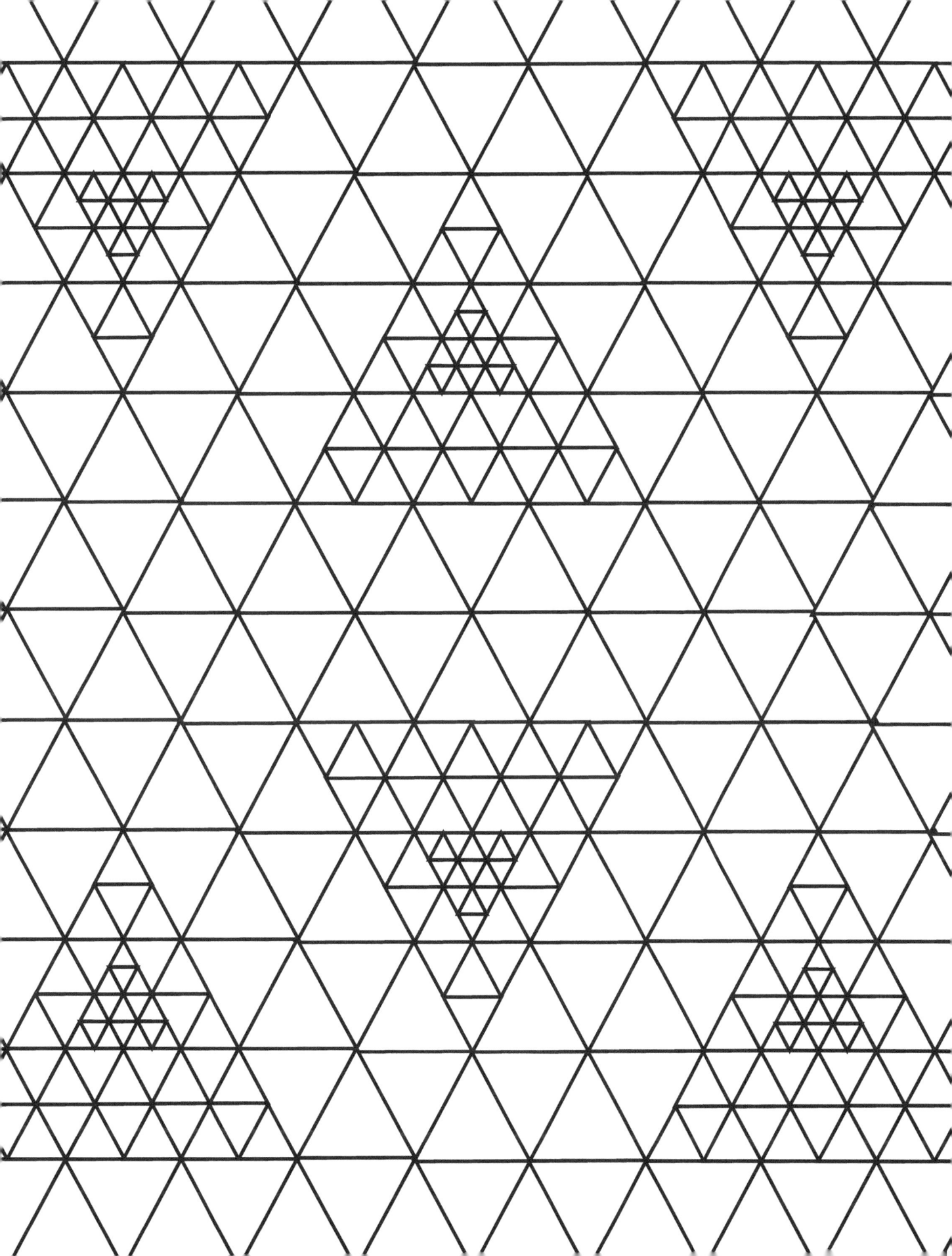

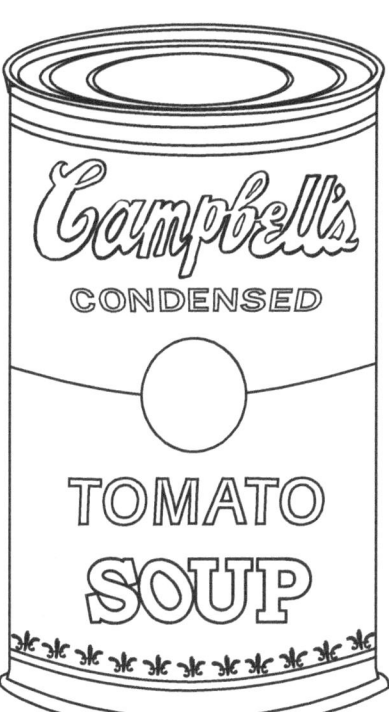
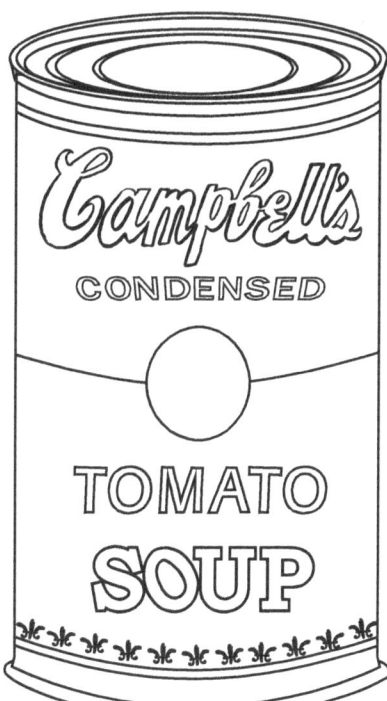
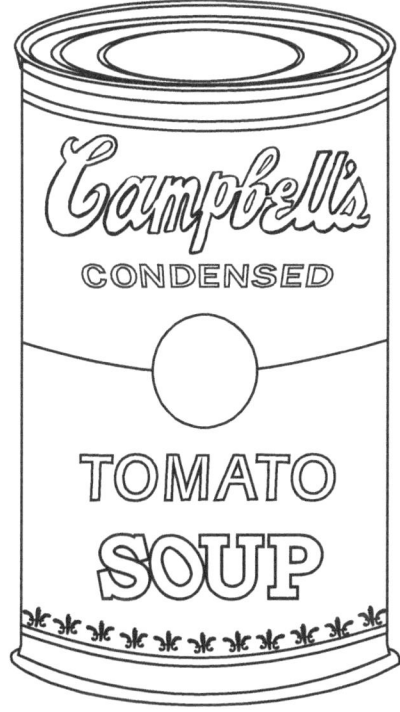
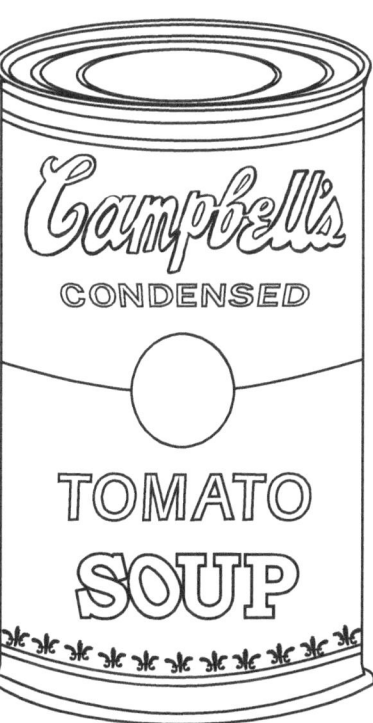

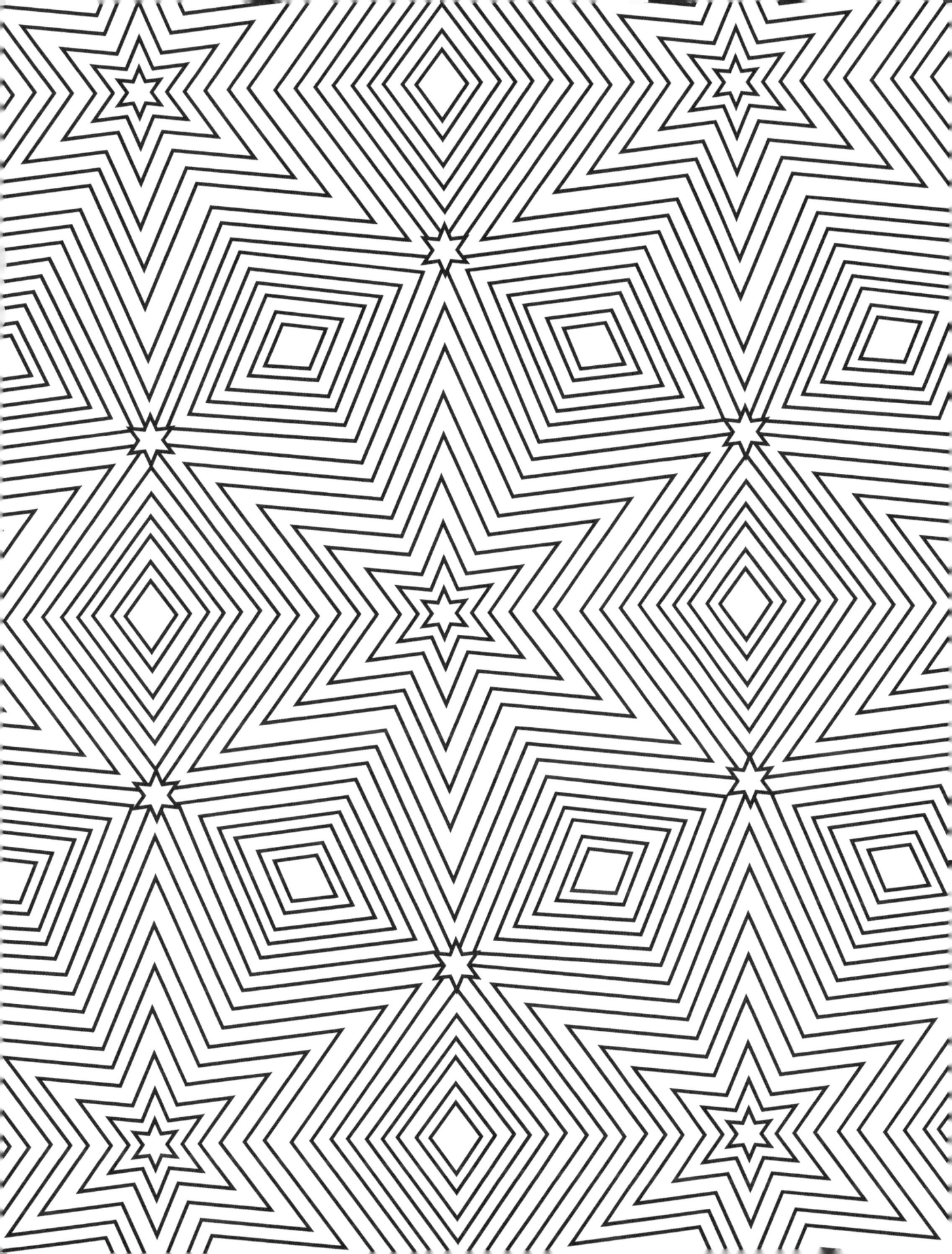

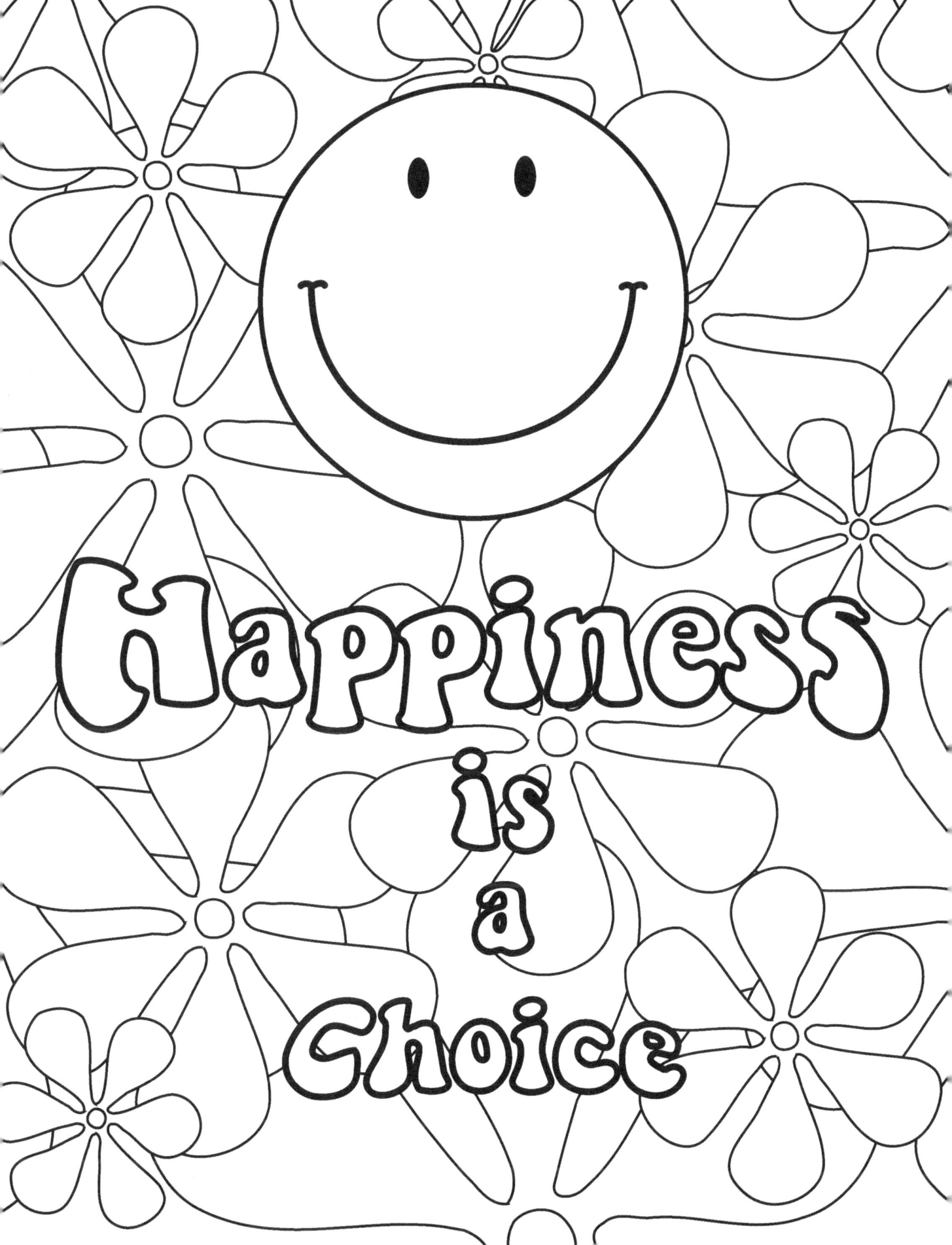